EASY STEW COOKBOOK

The Complete Cookbook To Learn How To Make Stew Guide With Over 100 Delicious And Tasty Stew Recipes

© 2019 Carrie Anderson

Contents

STEW

A stew has been depicted as a variety of nourishments cooked in fluid inside a compartment with a cover. Stews are typically produced using a few fixings and might be named for the most significant of these, for instance, hamburger stew; for its place, of course, as in Irish stew; or for the pot where it is cooked, as in Rumanian ghiveci, named for the Turkish güveç, a pottery pot in which the stew is cooked.

"Stew" is said to originate from the old French word Easter, which means to encase. Most social gatherings have made a formula for a unique stew, and there is the same number of renditions of them as there are cooks to make them.

In the Western world, meat stews are ordered as "dark colored" or "white." This implies the meat is seared in fat before fluid is included for the darker stew; meat for the white stew isn't cooked in fat before fluid is included. Stews may contain meat, fish, or poultry; a significant number of them, in any case, are meatless. There is additionally at times a barely recognizable difference among stews and soups. Stews are normally thick, some so thick that they should be served on a plate and eaten with a fork. Others are served in soup bowls. Stews regularly have a few strong nourishment fixings. An exemption is a fish stew, for example, clam or lobster stew, which contains crisp fish, milk, and oftentimes margarine.

Stews are ordinarily viewed as "comfort" nourishments, ordinary dishes served to family or dear companions in a personal setting, as opposed to as toll in an increasingly open setting or at uncommon events. A special case would be big à la bourguignonne, normally alluded to as hamburger burgundy in the US, a dish that is viewed as remarkable enough to be served to a visitor. This stew is made with meat, little onions, mushrooms, wine, and herbs. M. F. K. Fisher once composed that stews can be sufficient to be haute cooking, or the inverse, a feast fit for the most minimal echelon of society, the detained.

There are a few significant favorable circumstances to stews: Less delicate cuts of meat can be kneaded with the long, clammy cooking; progressively costly fixings that might be accessible just in modest quantities can be extended by including more affordable nourishments; meat cut in little pieces cooks quicker; and one-pot cooking monitors fuel and makes cleanup simpler. Stews might be cooked over a range, in a broiler, over an open fire, or in an electric Simmering pot.

Beef Stew Recipe Step By Step

Step 1: Ingredients:

- 1-2 pounds beef stew meat
- 3 stalks of celery
- 3-6 potatoes (3 if they're large, 6 if they're small)
- 4 carrots
- 1 onion
- 1/2 - 1 cup frozen peas (optional)
- 3-4 cloves garlic
- 4 tablespoons tomato paste
- 1/4 cup soy sauce
- 8 cups of liquid (make sure to make at least 2 cups of beef stock!)
- 2 tablespoons cornstarch
- 1-2 teaspoons dried thyme
- 2 bay leaves (if you have them on hand, I didn't!)
- Flour for coating the beef
- Freshly ground black pepper

Significant things to note:

1.Soy sauce may appear to be strange, yet we're utilizing it as opposed to including salt! It includes a profundity of flavor you can't accomplish with salt alone and I incline toward it considerably more than utilizing worcestershire sauce.

2.Beef stock is unquestionably required for enhance. I ordinarily purchase low sodium or no salt included meat stock so I can control the salt substance. I prescribe utilizing at least two cups of hamburger stock in the fluids. 6-8 cups of hamburger stock will give the best flavor, however it's progressively costly to do, which is the reason I typically evade it. :)

3.Don't spend an excessive amount of cash on the meat for this - we'll be cooking it so long it ought to get delicate and have season regardless. I simply purchase anything marked "stew meat" and utilize that - it's ordinarily under $5.

4.Swap the veggies as important. You could forget about the potatoes and go for another root vegetable, include more carrots, reduce the measure of celery. Do whatever you like, as long as despite everything you have some aromatics. (celery, onion, garlic)

5.Red wine or a dull, hefty brew are likewise welcome augmentations to hamburger stew - I'd state around 1/2 - 1 cup is a decent add up to begin with

Stage 2: Cooking in a Weight Cooker Versus Stovetop Versus Moderate Cooker

The means are basically the equivalent for each procedure, however there are some little contrasts.

In a weight cooker:

All out time: 45 minutes

Everything can truly go in on the double - simply hold off on the cornstarch until the stew is cooked. It will take 25 minutes at high strain to be done - brisk discharge the weight toward the end.

On the stovetop:

Complete time: 3.5 hours

Make a point to utilize a major, huge pot. You will need to stew the meat, onion, celery, garlic, soy sauce, tomato glue without anyone else for at any rate two hours. Try not to include the potatoes and carrots immediately - they'll separate excessively! When the meat is pleasant and delicate, don't hesitate to include the carrots and potatoes and stew for another 30-45 minutes. At that point you can change the seasonings and add cornstarch to thicken.

In the moderate cooker:

All out time: 8-9 hours

At the point when you cook this in the slow cooker, make a point to not avoid the carmelizing/shooting steps. I've done it and the taste was off. Darker the meat and put it in the slow cooker, and afterward saute the onions, celery and garlic alongside the thyme and tomato glue. Include those in the cockpit too. You can include the potatoes and carrots immediately in the event that you have to. (Despite the fact that I need to concede they have better surface when included part of the way through or considerably later!) I've let meat stew away throughout the day while I've been grinding away and the carrots and potatoes were still alright! You'll need to cook it on low for in any event 8 hours or until the meat is delicate. When it's prepared, you can include the cornstarch, thicken and serve.

Stage 3: Cut Up the Veggies!

It's good to cut the celery and onions all the more fine, and leave the carrots and potatoes in large pieces.

If your celery has leaves - use them! They're yummy.

Stage 4: Trim and Flour the Meat

Take sometime and trim off any silverskin you see or immense pieces of fat. And chop every one of the pieces down the to same size.

When that is done, cover the hamburger generously with pepper and afterward toss two or three bunches of flour on it also and blend it around until each piece is pleasant and covered.

We aren't utilizing any salt at this part since we'll add soy sauce to the cooking fluid!

Stage 5: Darken the Meat and saute the Veg

In case you're utilizing a weight cooker or doing this on the stove top, do this in the cooking vessel! In case you're cooking in the moderate cooker, you'll have to do this in a different dish.

Warmth a smidgen of oil over medium high warmth until it sparkles. At that point drop in the floured meat and cook until it's delicately sautéed and doesn't smell of crude flour any longer. This should take just a couple of moments - it'll simply rely upon how packed your pot is.

When it's set, include the celery, onions and garlic and blend well. Cook these, blending regularly, until the onions start to get somewhat translucent.

Stage 6: Include the Tomato Glue/thyme

When the veggies are getting delicate, include your tomato glue and thyme. Blend this around and let it cook until the thyme gets fragrant.

Stage 7: Include the Potatoes and Carrots!

Include them in and mix them around so everything is pleasantly covered with the seasonings.

Recall that in case you're cooking on the stovetop or in a moderate cooker, it could be smarter to hold on to include them in later.

Stage 8: Include the Stock, Water and Soy Sauce and Cook!

Include your fluids alongside 1/4 cup soy sauce. Blend well and afterward spread!

In a weight cooker you'll complete 25 minutes at high weight and afterward speedy discharge the weight.

On the stove you'll need to stew it over low warmth for at any rate two hours - make a point to mix occasionally!

In the moderate cooker, set it to low and leave it for eight hours.

Stage 9: Altering Seasonings and Including Soy Sauce

When you're finished cooking, taste for seasonings. Now you can include somewhat more soy sauce or tomato glue, more thyme or some dark pepper.

Additionally, in the event that you notice your hamburger stew has loads of fat coasting on top, don't hesitate to skim it off with a spoon

Stage 10: Thicken It!

Put two tablespoons of cornstarch in a little bowl or cup. Include around 1/4 cup of hot stock from the stew into the cornstarch and blend well in with a fork or whisk. You don't need any bunches!

When the cornstarch has broken down, empty the blend into the stew.

Turn up the warmth and cook for a couple of moments until pleasant and thick! What's more, if it's as yet not thick enough - include more cornstarch. Simply try to let it bubble for a couple of moments each time you include cornstarch so you realize how thick it is.

Stage 11: If You Need Peas, Include Them Now!

Mood killer the warmth and include your solidified peas. You would prefer not to overcook them so they get soft. :)

They just need two or three minutes in the warm stew to cook.

Stage 12: Enjoy!

Best presented with dried up meat and potatoes. Great with Parmesan cheddar and hot sauce!

Delicious and Tasty Stew Recipes

1.Old-fashioned Slow Cooker Beef Stew

Ingredients

- 3/4 cup all-purpose flour
- 1 1/2 teaspoons paprika (divided)
- 1 teaspoon garlic powder
- 2 pounds stew beef (lean chuck)
- 2 tablespoons vegetable oil
- 1 large onion (cut into chunks)
- 1 clove garlic (minced)
- 2 cups beef stock (unsalted or low sodium)
- 1 teaspoon salt (or to taste)
- 1 tablespoon lemon juice
- 1 teaspoon granulated sugar
- 1 teaspoon Worcestershire sauce
- 1/2 teaspoon freshly ground black pepper
- 2 bay leaves (medium-sized)
- 6 carrots (cut into 1/2-inch pieces)
- 6 medium potatoes (cut into 1/2-inch pieces)
- 1/3 cup cold water
- 3 tablespoons flour

Instructions

1. Gather the ingredients.
2. Combine the 3/4 cup of flour, 1 teaspoon of paprika, and the garlic powder in a food storage bag; add stew beef and toss to coat.
3. Heat the vegetable oil or olive oil in a large skillet over medium-high heat.
4. Brown the seasoned and coated beef in the hot oil, turning to sear the beef on all sides. Transfer the browned beef to the crockery insert of a slow cooker.
5. Add the onion, garlic, stock, salt, lemon juice, sugar, Worcestershire sauce, the remaining 1/2 teaspoon of paprika, the black pepper, bay leaves, carrots, and potatoes. See the variations below for other possible vegetable additions.

6. Cook the beef stew on the LOW setting for about 7 to 9 hours, or until the beef and vegetables are tender. Alternatively, cook the stew on HIGH for about 3 to 4 hours.
7. About 30 minutes before serving, combine the 3 tablespoons of flour and water; stir to make a smooth paste.
8. Add the flour and water mixture to the crock pot. Turn the heat setting to high and cook for about 20 to 30 minutes, or until the broth has thickened.

2.Classic Slow Cooker Beef Stew

Ingredients

- 10 small new potatoes (halved, unpeeled)
- 12 small whole pearl onions (peeled, fresh or frozen, thawed)
- 8 ounces baby carrots
- 1 red or green bell pepper (seeded, cut into 1-inch pieces)
- 1 1/2 pounds stew beef (cut into 1-inch cubes)
- 2 cups beef broth
- 1/2 teaspoon oregano (dried leaf)
- 1/4 teaspoon paprika
- 1 tablespoon parsley (fresh, chopped) or 1 teaspoon parsley (flakes, dried)
- 1 tablespoon Worcestershire sauce
- 1/2 teaspoon salt
- 1/8 teaspoon pepper
- 3 tablespoons cornstarch
- 3 tablespoons cold water

Instructions

1. Place the halved potatoes, onions, and baby carrots in the slow cooker. Add bell pepper and beef.
2. In a small bowl combine the beef broth, oregano, paprika, parsley, Worcestershire sauce, salt, and pepper. Pour the mixture over meat and vegetables.

3. Cover and cook the stew on low for 8 to 10 hours.
4. Turn pot on high. In a small bowl, dissolve the cornstarch in the water. Stir into cooked stew mixture. Cover and continue cooking the stew on high for 15 to 20 minutes or until thickened, stirring occasionally.

3.Slow Cooker Beef Stew

Ingredients

- 1 pound stew beef (cut into 1-inch cubes)
- 1 (10 3/4 oz) can condensed tomato soup
- 1 tablespoon tomato paste
- 1/2 cup water
- 1 tablespoon Gravy Master (or Kitchen Bouquet*)
- 3 medium potatoes (cubed)
- 3 medium carrots (peeled and diced)
- 1/4 cup chopped onion
- 1/2 teaspoon seasoned salt
- 1/2 teaspoon black pepper
- 1 cup frozen peas (add last before serving)

Instructions

1. Combine the stew beef, tomato soup, tomato paste, water, Gravy Master, potatoes, carrots, onion, seasoned salt, and pepper in the slow cooker.
2. Cover and cook on LOW for about 8 to 10 hours.
3. Add the peas in the last 30 minutes.

4.Slow Cooker Beef Stew With Sweet Potatoes

Ingredients

- 1 1/2 pounds lean stewing beef
- 3 tablespoons all-purpose flour
- 1/4 teaspoon kosher salt
- 1/4 teaspoon black pepper
- 1 large onion (or 2 medium, halved and cut into 1/4-inch slices)
- 1 tablespoon vegetable oil
- 2 medium sweet potatoes (or 1 if very large)
- 1/2 cup beef stock (homemade, canned, or from bouillon or base)
- 1/4 to 1/2 teaspoon cinnamon
- 1/2 to 1 cup peas (frozen, or green beans, thawed)
- Salt (to taste)
- Black pepper (to taste)
- *Optional:* 1 tablespoon flour (mixed with 2 tablespoons water)
- *Garnish:* fresh chopped parsley or cilantro

Instructions

1. Gather the ingredients.
2. Cut the stewing beef into bite-size pieces.
3. In a bowl or a paper bag or food storage bag, toss the stew beef with the flour and 1/4 teaspoon each salt and pepper.
4. Heat the vegetable oil in a large skillet or sauté pan over medium-high heat. Add the coated beef cubes and sliced onion to the pan and cook, stirring, until the beef is well browned.
5. Peel the sweet potato and cut into 1 to 1 1/2-inch cubes. You should have about 2 1/2 to 3 cups of cubes.
6. Place the sweet potato cubes in the crock pot; add beef and onions.
7. Mix beef broth with cinnamon and pour over beef mixture.
8. Cover and cook on low 7 to 9 hours, or until the beef is tender.
9. Taste and adjust seasonings with salt and pepper, as needed.
10. Add peas or green beans during the last 15 to 20 minutes.
11. If you would like to thicken the stew, combine the flour and water and stir to make a smooth paste. Add to the stew and turn to HIGH. Cook for about 10 minutes longer, or until thickened.

12. Serve this beef stew with biscuits or crusty bread.
13. Enjoy!

5. Beef and Barley Stew

Ingredients

- 4 slices bacon (diced)
- 1 tablespoon extra virgin olive oil
- 1 1/2 pounds beef chuck (lean stewing beef, cut into small pieces)
- 3 tablespoons all-purpose flour
- 1/2 teaspoon salt
- 1/8 teaspoon pepper
- 8 ounces mushrooms (sliced)
- 1 cup sliced celery
- 1 1/2 cups onion (chopped)
- 6 cups beef stock
- 1 bay leaf
- 1/3 cup pearled barley
- 2 cups carrot (sliced)
- 2 cups turnip (diced)
- 1 large potato (cut into cubes)
- 1 cup green peas (frozen, thawed)
- 2 tablespoons flour
- 2 tablespoons cold water

Instructions

1. Gather the ingredients.
2. Cook the bacon over medium-low heat in a large stockpot or Dutch oven until almost crisp.
3. Toss the stew beef pieces with the flour, salt, and pepper. Add the beef to the bacon mixture and cook for about 3 minutes, stirring frequently.
4. Add the olive oil along with the mushrooms, celery, and onion. Cook over medium heat, frequently stirring until the onion is translucent and the beef has browned nicely.
5. Add the beef stock and bay leaf and bring to a boil over high heat. Cover the pan, reduce the heat to low, and simmer for 45 minutes.

6. Add the barley, carrots, and turnip. Reduce heat to low. Cover and simmer for 25 minutes.
7. Add potatoes and simmer for about 25 minutes longer, or until the vegetables and meat are tender.
8. Add thawed the peas to the stew and cook for about 10 minutes longer.
9. To thicken the stew, combine the 2 tablespoons of flour with 2 tablespoons of cold water. Whisk until smooth. Stir the flour mixture into the stew. Continue cooking until thickened, stirring constantly.
10. Serve and enjoy!

6.Crock Pot Beef, Vegetable, and Barley Stew

Ingredients

- 1/2 pound of stew beef (cut into small pieces)
- 1 or 2 meaty beef shanks
- 2 cups carrots (sliced thin)
- 2 ribs celery (with tops, sliced)
- 1 large onion (diced)
- 1 cup frozen cut green beans
- 1 (14.5-ounce) can diced tomatoes
- *Optional:* 3/4 cup frozen lima beans
- 1 1/2 teaspoons salt
- 2 cloves garlic (minced)
- 1 bay leaf
- 2 medium potatoes (peeled and cubed)
- 2 teaspoons dried basil
- 1 tablespoon dried parsley
- 4 to 5 cups beef broth (preferably low sodium)
- 1/4 cup barley
- 1 1/2 cups frozen peas (thawed under cold running water)

Instructions

1. Gather the ingredients.
2. Add everything but the barley and peas to the 5 to 6-quart crock pot. Add water to within 1 1/2 inches of the top and stir. Cook on LOW for 6 to 8 hours, or until the beef is tender. Remove the beef shanks to a plate and cut the meat from the bones. Discard the bones.
3. Add the beef back to the slow cooker along with the barley. Increase the heat to HIGH and cook for about 1 hour and 45 minutes longer. Add the thawed peas and

continue cooking on HIGH for about 15 minutes longer, or until the barley is tender.
4. Serve and enjoy!

7.Vegetable Beef and Barley Stew

Ingredients

- 1 pound of beef chuck (stewing beef)
- 1 large onion
- 1 tablespoon extra virgin olive oil
- 6 medium carrots
- 1/2 cup chopped celery
- 2 (14.5-ounce) cans tomatoes (undrained)
- 4 beef bouillon cubes (or equivalent base or granules)
- 1 (12-ounce) can V-8 juice
- 1/4 cup pearl barley
- 1 tablespoon Worcestershire sauce
- 1 teaspoon garlic powder
- 1 (15 oz.) can green beans, drained
- Salt and freshly ground black pepper, to taste

Instructions

1. Gather the ingredients.
2. Cut the beef into 1/2 inch cubes or bite-size pieces.
3. Peel the onion and cut it into 1/4 inch dice.
4. Heat the oil in a Dutch oven or stockpot over medium heat.
5. When the oil is hot and shimmering, add the beef cubes and chopped onion and cook, stirring, until the beef has browned and the onion is tender.
6. Meanwhile, peel the carrots and slice thinly.
7. Add the carrots and celery to the beef mixture along with the tomatoes, beef base or bouillon, V-8 juice, barley, Worcestershire sauce, and garlic powder. Cover and cook for about 1 hour.
8. Add the drained green beans about 10 minutes before the soup is ready.
9. Taste the soup and add salt and pepper, as needed.
10. Enjoy!

8.Crock Pot Country Beef Stew

Ingredients

- 2 pounds stewing beef
- 4 medium carrots
- 3 onions
- 6 potatoes (medium)
- 3 ribs celery
- 2 (14.5-ounce) cans tomatoes (diced)
- 1 cup beef stock (preferably unsalted or low sodium)
- 6 tablespoons quick-cooking tapioca
- 3 tablespoons Worcestershire sauce
- 2 bay leaves
- Dash ground allspice
- 1/4 teaspoon dried marjoram (or oregano)
- 1/4 teaspoon dried thyme (or to taste)
- Kosher salt and freshly ground black pepper (to taste)
- 1 (10-ounce) package frozen green peas (thawed)

Instructions

1. Cut the beef into 1-inch cubes.
2. Peel the carrots and slice them into 1//4 to 1/2-inch rounds.
3. Peel and chop the onions.
4. Peel the potatoes and cut them into 1-inch cubes.
5. Slice the celery.
6. Combine the chopped and sliced vegetables in the slow cooker with the beef, tomatoes, beef stock, tapioca, Worcestershire sauce, and bay leaves.
7. Cover and cook on low for 7 to 9 hours.
8. Taste the stew and add the allspice, marjoram, thyme, salt, and pepper, as needed
9. Turn to high and add frozen peas about 20 minutes before serving.

9.Crock Pot Barbecue Beef Stew

Ingredients

- 1 1/2 pounds beef chuck (stewing beef)
- 3 tablespoons vegetable oil
- 1 cup chopped onion
- 1/2 cup green pepper (chopped)
- 1 clove garlic (large, minced)
- 1/2 teaspoon salt
- 1/8 teaspoon pepper
- 2 cups beef stock (preferably unsalted or low sodium)
- 1 (14.5-ounce) can tomatoes
- 1 (4-ounce) can mushrooms (drained)
- 1/3 cup barbecue sauce
- 3 tablespoons cornstarch
- 1/4 cup cold water

Instructions

1. Cut the beef into bite-si
2. ze cubes (1/2-inch to 1-inch).
3. Heat the vegetable oil in a skillet over medium-high heat. Cook the beef and onion in the hot oil until beef is browned on all sides, stirring constantly.
4. Reduce the heat to medium. Add the garlic and chopped green pepper and cook for 1 minute longer.
5. Transfer the beef mixture to the slow cooker. Add the salt, pepper, beef stock, tomatoes, mushrooms, and barbecue sauce. Cover and cook on low for about 7 to 9 hours, or until the beef is very tender.
6. Mix 2 tablespoons of cornstarch with the cold water until smooth and well blended. Stir the cornstarch slurry stir into the stew and continue to cook for 10 to 20 minutes, or until thickened..

10.Easy Crock Pot Beef and Mushroom Stew

Ingredients

- 1 1/2 pounds beef chuck (lean, or use round steak)
- 4 (10 3/4-ounce) cans condensed cream of mushroom soup
- 1 (4-ounce) can sliced mushrooms (undrained)
- Optional: dash ground ginger
- 5 cloves garlic (coarsely chopped)
- 1/2 teaspoon dried leaf oregano
- 1/2 teaspoon dried leaf basil
- 1/2 teaspoon onion powder
- 1/4 cup water
- 1/2 teaspoon ground black pepper
- Salt, to taste

Instructions

1. Cut the beef into 1/2-inch to 1-inch cubes.
2. Put the beef cubes in the slow cooker along with the condensed soup, mushrooms, ginger, garlic, oregano, basil, onion powder, water, and black pepper.
3. Cover the pot and cook on low for 7 to 9 hours.
4. Serve the beef and sauce with mashed potatoes, rice, or noodles.

11.Slow Cooker Beef and Mushroom Stew

Ingredients

- 1 1/2 pounds beef chuck (or cut-up stewing beef)
- 1 (10 3/4-ounce) can condensed French onion soup
- 1/2 cup red wine (burgundy / pinot noir, cabernet, etc.)
- 4 to 5 medium potatoes (cubed)
- 2 medium carrots (sliced)
- 12 to 16 ounces fresh mushrooms
- 1 bay leaf
- 1/2 teaspoon kosher salt (or to taste)

- 1/4 teaspoon freshly ground black pepper
- Small sprig of rosemary (or a pinch of dried, crumbled)
- 1 (14.5-ounce) can diced tomatoes
- 3 tablespoons flour
- 3 tablespoons cold water

Instructions

1. Gather the ingredients.
2. Cut the beef into 1/2-inch to 1-inch pieces.
3. Combine the stewing beef, condensed onion soup, red wine, potatoes, carrots, mushrooms, bay leaf, salt, pepper, and rosemary.
4. Cover and cook on low for 7 to 9 hours; add the tomatoes about 45 minutes to an hour before the stew is ready.
5. About 15 to 20 minutes before the stew is ready, combine the flour and cold water in a small bowl. Whisk or stir until smooth and well blended. Add the flour and water mixture to the stew and stir to blend. Taste and adjust seasonings with more salt and pepper, if needed.
6. Serve with biscuits, French bread, or crusty rolls.
7. Enjoy!

12.Beef Stew With Vegetables and Tomatoes

Ingredients

- **For the Beef:**
- 1/3 cup all-purpose flour
- 1/2 teaspoon salt
- 1/4 teaspoon black pepper
- 2 pounds beef chuck (lean, cut into 1/2-inch pieces)
- **For the Sauce:**
- 3 tablespoons extra virgin olive oil
- 1/2 cup chopped onion
- 2 ribs celery (cleaned, sliced thinly)
- 2 cloves garlic (minced)
- 2 (14.5 oz) cans diced tomatoes
- 1/2 cup dry red wine (burgundy, pinot noir, or cabernet)
- 2 cups beef broth

- 1/2 teaspoon black pepper (freshly ground)
- 1 teaspoon dried leaf thyme
- 1 cup potatoes (peeled, diced)
- 1/2 cup carrots (diced)
- Optional: 1/2 cup diced rutabaga (or turnip)
- **For Sauce Thickening:**
- 3 tablespoons flour
- 1/4 cup water (cold)
- Garnish: Parsley (chopped)

Instructions

1. Gather the ingredients.
2. In a large bowl, mix the beef with the flour, salt, and pepper. Toss until well coated.
3. In a large Dutch oven or saucepan, heat the olive oil over medium heat. Add the seasoned beef and cook, stirring, until browned.
4. Add the onion and celery and continue cooking until the onion is soft and fragrant.
5. Add the garlic, tomatoes, wine, and beef broth. Bring to a boil; reduce heat, cover, and simmer for 1 1/2 hours.
6. Once the cooking time has passed, add the pepper, thyme, potatoes, carrots, and rutabaga or turnip. Cover and simmer for 35 to 45 minutes longer, or until all vegetables are tender.
7. In a small bowl mix the flour and cold water and add to the pot. Continue cooking, stirring, until the sauce has thickened, for about 10 minutes.
8. Transfer to serving bowls and garnish with parsley, if using.
9. Serve hot and enjoy!

13.Beef Stew With Carrots and Potatoes

Ingredients

- 2 pounds beef chuck (lean, stewing beef)
- 2 tablespoons vegetable oil
- 4 medium carrots
- 4 medium onions
- 4 medium potatoes
- 1 (10 1/2-ounce) can condensed beef broth
- 2 cups water
- 3/4 teaspoon Worcestershire sauce

- 1/2 teaspoon salt, or to taste
- Dash pepper
- 4 whole cloves
- 3 tablespoons flour
- 3 tablespoons cold water

Instructions

1. Pat the beef with paper towels to dry and then cut it into bite-size cubes.
2. Heat the vegetable oil in a Dutch oven or stockpot over medium-high heat.
3. Add the beef cubes to the pan and cook until browned, stirring and turning frequently.
4. Slice the carrots into 1-inch rounds. Cut the onions into chunks, and cut the potatoes into 1-inch cubes.
5. Add the prepared vegetables to the beef along with the beef broth, water, Worcestershire sauce, salt, and pepper.
6. Tie the cloves in a small cheesecloth bag and add to the stew. If you don't have cheesecloth, a tea infuser will work.
7. Cover the pan and simmer the stew for 1 1/2 hours. Drain off the liquid into a saucepan.
8. In a small bowl, mix the flour with the cold water until smooth and then blend into the hot liquid in the saucepan.
9. Cook, stirring constantly until thickened.
10. Add the thickened broth to the meat and vegetable mixture. Remove the cloves.

14. Vegetable Beef Stew

Ingredients

- 2 pounds stewing beef (or a chuck roast)
- 2 to 3 teaspoons vegetable oil
- 1/2 teaspoon seasoned salt
- 1 cup onions (chopped)
- 1 can/10 1/2 ounces condensed beef broth (or concentrated rich beef stock)
- 3 cups potatoes (diced)
- 2 cups carrots (diced)
- 2 ribs celery (cut into 1/2-inch pieces)
- 2 tablespoons all-purpose flour
- 1/3 cup water (cold)

- Seasoned salt to taste
- Black pepper to taste

Instructions

1. Cut the beef into small, bite-sized cubes.
2. Heat the vegetable oil in a Dutch oven or large kettle; add the beef, seasoned salt, and chopped onions. Cook, turning frequently, over medium heat for about 10 to 15 minutes, until the meat is browned on all sides and chopped onions are tender. Drain off excess fat if necessary.
3. Add the beef broth and some hot water to the pot until the liquid level is about 1 inch above the beef. Cover and reduce heat to low. Cover and simmer for 1 1/2 to 2 hours or until the meat is tender.
4. Add the potatoes, carrots, and celery. Cover and cook, stirring occasionally, for 20 to 30 minutes longer, until vegetables are tender.
5. To thicken the stew, combine the flour with 1/3 cup cold water; stir until smooth. Gently stir flour mixture into the pot a little at a time, using as much as needed to make the stew as thick as you like it.
6. Add pepper and taste for seasonings, adding more seasoned salt if necessary.

15.Crock Pot Country Beef Stew

Ingredients

- 2 pounds stewing beef
- 4 medium carrots
- 3 onions
- 6 potatoes (medium)
- 3 ribs celery
- 2 (14.5-ounce) cans tomatoes (diced)
- 1 cup beef stock (preferably unsalted or low sodium)
- 6 tablespoons quick-cooking tapioca
- 3 tablespoons Worcestershire sauce
- 2 bay leaves
- Dash ground allspice
- 1/4 teaspoon dried marjoram (or oregano)
- 1/4 teaspoon dried thyme (or to taste)
- Kosher salt and freshly ground black pepper (to taste)
- 1 (10-ounce) package frozen green peas (thawed)

Instructions

1. Cut the beef into 1-inch cubes.
2. Peel the carrots and slice them into 1//4 to 1/2-inch rounds.
3. Peel and chop the onions.
4. Peel the potatoes and cut them into 1-inch cubes.
5. Slice the celery.
6. Combine the chopped and sliced vegetables in the slow cooker with the beef, tomatoes, beef stock, tapioca, Worcestershire sauce, and bay leaves.
7. Cover and cook on low for 7 to 9 hours.
8. Taste the stew and add the allspice, marjoram, thyme, salt, and pepper, as needed
9. Turn to high and add frozen peas about 20 minutes before serving.

16.Crockpot Easy Beef Stew

Ingredients

- 6 medium red potatoes
- 1 1/2 pounds beef sirloin tip (cut into 1" cubes)
- 1/3 cup flour
- Optional: salt and pepper (to taste)
- 1 (14-ounce) can diced tomatoes (undrained)
- 2 cups beef stock
- 3 cups frozen stir-fry bell peppers and onions

Instructions

1. Scrub the potatoes and cut each into quarters. Place the potatoes in the bottom of a 4-quart slow cooker.

2. Mix the flour, salt, and pepper and toss with the cubed beef to coat. Add the coated beef to the crockpot. Add undrained tomatoes and beef stock and stir gently.
3. Cover the crockpot and cook on low for 7 to 8 hours until the beef and potatoes are tender. Add stir-fry vegetables. Cover the slow cooker again and cook on low for 30 to 40 minutes until the vegetables are hot and tender.
4. You can thicken this mixture if you'd like by adding about a tablespoon or two of cornstarch or flour to about 1/4 cup of water or beef broth. Mix well until the flour has dissolved. Stir this mixture into the stew in the crockpot, cover, and cook on high for 10 to 15 minutes or until the stew has thickened.

17.Healthy Crockpot Beef Stew

Ingredients

- 1 1/2 pounds sirloin tip (cut into 1 1/2" cubes)
- 2 tablespoons flour
- 1/4 teaspoon salt
- 1/8 teaspoon pepper
- 1/2 cup red wine or beef broth
- 2 cups low sodium beef broth
- 2 (14-ounce) cans diced tomatoes (Italian seasoned, undrained)
- 3 cloves garlic (minced)
- 1 onion (chopped)
- 2 cups baby carrots
- 1 (9-ounce) package frozen cut green beans (thawed)
- 9 ounces fettuccine (fresh, cut in half)

Instructions

1. Toss the cubed beef with the flour, salt, and pepper and place in a 3 1/2 quart or larger crockpot.
2. Add red wine or beef broth, remaining beef broth, diced tomatoes, garlic, onion, and baby carrots and mix well.
3. Cover the slow cooker and cook on low for 8 to 9 hours until the beef is tender.
4. Stir in the green beans and the pasta. Increase heat to high and cover the crockpot. Cook for 10 to 13 minutes longer until the pasta is tender.
5. If you have a new, hotter cooking crockpot, cook on low for 6 1/2 to 8 hours until the beef is tender, then add the pasta and beans.

6. Serve immediately.

18.Crockpot Meatball and Potato Stew

Ingredients

- 1-pound package frozen meatballs
- 4 russet or Yukon Gold potatoes, peeled and sliced or cubed
- 1 (16 ounce) bag baby carrots
- 1 onion, chopped
- 3 cloves garlic, sliced
- 3 (14 ounce) cans ready to serve beef broth
- 1 cup water
- 1 tablespoon dried parsley flakes
- 1 teaspoon dried marjoram leaves
- 1 teaspoon dried basil leaves
- 1/2 teaspoon salt
- 1/8 teaspoon pepper
- 1 (12 ounce) can evaporated milk
- 3 tablespoons cornstarch

Instructions

1. Spray a 4 or 5-quart crockpot with nonstick cooking spray.
2. Place meatballs, potatoes, baby carrots, onion, and garlic in the slow cooker. Add broth, water, parsley, marjoram, basil, salt, and pepper and mix gently.
3. Cover the crockpot and cook on low for 9 to 11 hours.
4. Mix evaporated milk and cornstarch; add during last hour and cook until thoroughly heated and thickened. 4 to 6 servings
5. If you have a new hotter cooking crockpot cook on low for 6 to 8 hours.

19.Crock Pot Pork and Sweet Potato Stew

Ingredients

- 1 pound boneless pork shoulder (cut into 1" cubes)
- 3 cups peeled (cubed sweet potatoes)
- 2 apples (cored and chopped)
- 1 onion (chopped)
- 1 teaspoon dried thyme leaves
- 1/4 teaspoon pepper
- 1/2 teaspoon salt
- 3 cups apple juice
- 2 tablespoons cornstarch
- 1/4 cup water

Instructions

1. Layer the sweet potatoes, apples, and onion in a 4 to 5-quart slow cooker. Sprinkle the ingredients with thyme, salt, and pepper, then top with the pork cubes. Pour apple juice over all; do not stir.
2. Cover the crockpot and cook on low for 7 to 8 hours or until the meat and veggies are tender.
3. Then, in a small bowl, combine the cornstarch and water; stir well with a wire whisk until the mixture is smooth. Stir the cornstarch slurry into the stew; cover and cook on high for 15 minutes until thickened. Serve immediately.

20.Slow Cooker Pork Stew

Ingredients

- 2 pounds pork shoulder (boneless trimmed, cut into 3/4-inch cubes)
- 3 tablespoons flour
- 1 teaspoon salt
- 1/4 teaspoon dried thyme
- 1/4 teaspoon pepper
- 6 carrots (cut into 1/2-inch slices)

- 4 medium potatoes (cut into 3/4-inch cubes)
- 1 cup onion (chopped)
- 1 large apple (peeled, cored, and chopped)
- 2 cups apple cider
- 1 tablespoon vinegar
- 1/2 cup cold water
- 1/4 cup flour

Instructions

1. Gather the ingredients.
2. Combine the flour, salt, thyme, and pepper. Toss the spices with the meat.
3. Put the chopped-up vegetables (carrots, potatoes, and onions) and the apple into the slow-cooker.
4. Place the pork cubes on top.
5. Combine apple cider and vinegar, and pour it over the meat.
6. Place the lid on top of the slow cooker and set it on the low setting. Keep it on the low setting for 9 to 11 hours.
7. After that time, turn the slow cooker to high. Blend 1/4 cup flour and 1/2 cup cold water together, stirring them until the mixture is smooth (this will thicken the sauce).
8. Stir the flour and water into the hot liquid. Keep the crock pot on high, and cook it for 15 minutes longer, or until thickened.
9. Taste and adjust seasonings as desired.
10. Serve and enjoy!

21. Crock Pot Spanish-Style Pork Stew

Ingredients

- 1 medium onion
- 1 pound lean pork shoulder (also known as pork butt or Boston butt)
- 4 to 5 medium potatoes
- 1 green bell pepper (or use half green and half red)
- 2 tablespoons vegetable oil
- 1 (14.5 oz) can tomatoes (diced)
- 2 tablespoons vinegar
- 3 garlic cloves (crushed)
- 1 cup chicken stock (preferably low sodium or unsalted)

- 1 bay leaf
- Salt and pepper, to taste

Instructions

1. Chop the onion.
2. Cut the pork shoulder into large chunks.
3. Peel the potatoes and cut them into 1-inch pieces.
4. Slice the bell pepper in half lengthwise; remove the stem end along with the seeds and ribs and then slice thinly.
5. Heat the vegetable oil in a skillet over medium-high heat. Add the pork cubes and cook until well browned on all sides, turning frequently.
6. Put the onion in the slow cooker. Top with the browned pork, cubed potatoes, and bell pepper.
7. In a bowl, combine the tomatoes with the vinegar, garlic, chicken broth, and bay leaf. Pour over the pork.
8. Cover the pot and cook the stew on LOW for 7 to 9 hours, or until the pork is tender. Taste and adjust seasonings with salt and pepper, as needed.

22. Cazuela de Vaca (Beef and Pumpkin Stew)

Ingredients

- 1-pound package frozen meatballs
- 4 russet or Yukon Gold potatoes, peeled and sliced or cubed
- 1 (16 ounce) bag baby carrots
- 1 onion, chopped
- 3 cloves garlic, sliced
- 3 (14 ounce) cans ready to serve beef broth
- 1 cup water
- 1 tablespoon dried parsley flakes
- 1 teaspoon dried marjoram leaves
- 1 teaspoon dried basil leaves
- 1/2 teaspoon salt
- 1/8 teaspoon pepper
- 1 (12 ounce) can evaporated milk
- 3 tablespoons cornstarch

Directions

1. Cut the piece of beef into 6 large chunks (one per serving). Place the beef into a large saucepan; pour in the beef broth and water. Bring to a boil over high heat, then reduce heat to medium, cover, and simmer until nearly tender, 1 to 1 1/2 hours.
2. Stir the polenta into the stew along with the potatoes and onion. Cover and simmer for 15 minutes. Cut the pumpkin into 6, serving-sized pieces, and add to the stew along with the corn, carrot, bell pepper, celery, and leek; simmer until the vegetables are tender, adding more water if needed to barely cover. Stir in the oregano and paprika during the last 5 minutes.
3. Season to taste with salt and pepper. Ladle into serving bowls, and sprinkle with chopped cilantro.

23. Easy French Beef Burgundy Recipe

Ingredients

- 5 slices bacon (chopped)
- 1 cup yellow or white onions (chopped)
- 3 medium carrots (cut into 1/4-inch slices)
- 1/4 cup celery (finely chopped)
- 2 pounds beef chuck (cubed)
- 1/2 teaspoon salt
- 1/4 teaspoon ground black pepper
- 2 teaspoons dried parsley
- 1/2 teaspoon dried thyme
- 1/4 teaspoon dried crushed rosemary
- 1/16 teaspoon ground allspice (scant pinch)
- 1 tablespoon all-purpose flour
- 1 teaspoon tomato paste
- 1 1/2 cups mushrooms (cleaned, coarsely chopped)
- 1 cup burgundy (or dry red wine)
- 1/2 cup beef stock

Instructions

1. Gather the ingredients.
2. In a large saucepan over high heat, cook the bacon until it turns crisp. Transfer the bacon to a paper-towel-lined plate to drain.
3. Pour all but 2 tablespoons of bacon grease from the pan. Saute the onions, carrots, and celery in the bacon grease for 5 minutes, until the vegetables turn soft. Transfer them to a bowl with a slotted spoon and set it aside for a moment.

4. Season the beef with the salt and pepper and brown it in the remaining bacon grease. Once all sides of the beef are browned, sprinkle the parsley, thyme, rosemary, allspice, and flour over the beef.
5. Stir in the tomato paste and cook the spiced beef for 1 minute.
6. Add the mushrooms, cooked vegetables, crisped bacon, red wine, and beef stock, into the pan with the beef, and then cook the mixture over low heat, covered, for 1 hour and 15 minutes.

24.A Classic French Venison Stew

Ingredients

- 2 pounds venison (cubed)
- 1 cup yellow onions (or white onions, chopped)
- 3 medium carrots (cut into 1/4-inch slices)
- 1/4 cup celery (finely chopped)
- 3/4 teaspoon salt
- 1/2 teaspoon ground black pepper
- 2 teaspoons dried parsley
- 1/2 teaspoon dried thyme
- 1/4 teaspoon dried crushed rosemary
- 1 cup dry red wine
- 3/4 cup beef stock
- 5 slices bacon (chopped)
- 1 tablespoon all-purpose flour
- 1 teaspoon tomato paste
- 1 1/2 cups cleaned mushrooms

Instructions

1. Gather the ingredients.
2. Put the venison, onions, carrots, celery, salt, pepper, and the herbs in a glass bowl or casserole dish.
3. Pour the red wine and beef stock over the venison and marinate in the refrigerator for 8 hours, or overnight.
4. Drain the liquid marinade and reserve it for use later in this recipe.
5. In a large saucepan over high heat, cook the bacon until it turns crisp.
6. Transfer the bacon to a paper towel-lined plate to drain.
7. Pour all but 2 tablespoons of bacon grease from the pan. Sauté the onions, carrots, and celery in the bacon grease for 5 minutes, until the vegetables turn soft. Transfer them to a bowl with a slotted spoon and set it aside for a moment.

8. Toss the venison with the flour and brown it in the remaining bacon grease.
9. Once all sides of the meat are browned, stir in the tomato paste and cook the mixture for 1 minute.
10. Add the mushrooms, cooked vegetables, crisped bacon, and reserved marinade liquid into the pan with the browned venison.
11. Cook the mixture over low heat, covered, for 45 minutes to 1 hour. The venison stew is done when the meat and vegetables are tender and the sauce is thickened.
12. Serve the casserole with simple, fresh, green vegetables and a spoon or two of lovely mashed potatoes to soak up the juices.

25. Classic French Venison Bourguignon

Ingredients

- 3 cups dry red wine
- 2 cups strong beef stock
- 1/4 cup Cognac (or good quality brandy)
- 1 large yellow onion (chopped into large pieces)
- 2 carrots (peeled and cut into 2-inch-long pieces)
- 3 cloves garlic (crushed and chopped)
- 1/4 cup chopped fresh parsley
- 1 teaspoon dried thyme
- 1 teaspoon dried rosemary
- 10 black peppercorns
- 3 whole cloves
- 1 allspice berries
- 1 dried bay leaf
- 3 pounds venison chuck (shoulder cuts, cut into 2-inch chunks
- 1/2 pound bacon (cut into thick slices, and then coarsely chopped)
- 1 tablespoon butter
- 1 tablespoon tomato paste
- 2 tablespoons olive oil
- 1 pound pearl onions (peeled)
- 1 pound white mushrooms (wiped clean and bottoms trimmed)
- 1/2 teaspoon salt
- 1/4 teaspoon ground black pepper
- 1 tablespoon all-purpose flour

Instructions

1. Gather the ingredients.
2. In a large non-reactive container, combine the red wine, beef stock, Cognac, onion, carrots, garlic, parsley, thyme, rosemary, peppercorns, cloves, allspice, bay leaf, and venison pieces. Marinate the mixture for at least eight hours or overnight in the refrigerator.
3. Preheat an oven to 300 F. Remove the venison from the marinade and drain it on a clean kitchen towel. Using a slotted spoon, transfer the vegetables to a bowl and reserve the marinade liquid.
4. In a large Dutch oven set over medium-high heat, fry the bacon until it's crisp. Remove to a plate and let drain on a paper towel. Retain the grease in the pan.
5. Add the drained venison to the bacon fat and cook over high heat, often turning, until the venison is browned. Transfer the venison to a paper towel-lined plate.
6. Add the marinade vegetables to the fat and sauté them over medium-high heat, often stirring, for about 5 to 7 minutes. Drain any remaining fat. Stir in the tomato paste and allow it to cook for about 30 seconds. Gradually add the all of the reserved marinade liquid, continuously stirring to form a smooth sauce.
7. Return the venison and bacon to the Dutch oven and stir to combine the ingredients. Cover with a lid and cook in the preheated oven for three hours, until the venison is tender.
8. Using a slotted spoon, transfer the venison to a clean bowl. Strain and skim the fat from the sauce and pour it back into the Dutch oven, along with the venison.
9. In a large skillet over medium-high heat, sauté the pearl onions for about 10 minutes until they turn tender. Continue cooking them until most of the cooking liquid evaporates. Add the mushrooms, salt, and pepper to the pan and sauté them, along with the onions for 5 minutes.
10. Knead together the reserved tablespoon of softened butter and 1 tablespoon all-purpose flour to make a beurre manie, which is much like a roux. Stir the beurre manie into the simmering onion and mushroom mixture and cook it for 1 minute, until it thickens slightly. Add the thickened vegetable garnish to the Dutch oven and bring the stew to a simmer for 3 minutes.
11. Remove from the heat and serve hot.
12. Enjoy!

26.Easy Venison Stew

Ingredients

- 1 to 2 pounds venison roast
- Salt and pepper to taste
- 2 to 3 tablespoons all-purpose flour
- 2 tablespoons vegetable oil
- 8 ounces fresh sauteed mushrooms or canned mushroom pieces
- 1 can (10 3/4 ounces) condensed beefy mushroom soup or golden mushroom
- 1 can (10 3/4 ounces) beef noodle soup
- 1/2 teaspoon garlic powder
- *Optional:* 1/2 teaspoon onion powder
- 2 teaspoons Worcestershire sauce

Instructions

1. Gather the ingredients.
2. Trim the venison roast and cut it into 1-inch cubes.
3. Sprinkle the venison cubes with seasoned salt and pepper. Roll the pieces in flour to coat.
4. If you have a slow cooker with a saute feature, heat 2 tablespoons of olive oil in the slow cooker and sear the venison on all sides. Then remove and saute the mushrooms. If not, heat 2 tablespoons of oil in a skillet over high heat; sear venison pieces on all sides. Place the venison in the slow cooker.
5. If using fresh mushrooms, add a little more oil or butter to the skillet and saute the mushrooms, stirring, for about 4 to 5 minutes.
6. In a bowl, combine the soups with the sauteed or canned drained mushrooms; stir to blend. Season with garlic powder, onion powder, and Worcestershire sauce. Pour the mixture over the venison in the slow cooker.
7. Cover and cook on the low setting for 9 to 11 hours or on the high setting for about 4 1/2 to 5 1/2 hours or until the venison is tender.

Oven Instructions

1. Preheat the oven to 250 F.

2. Sear the seasoned and coated venison cubes in the skillet and transfer to a Dutch oven or casserole. Saute the fresh mushrooms, if using.
3. Combine the soups and the sauteed or canned drained mushrooms with the garlic powder, onion powder, and Worcestershire sauce. Pour over the venison.
4. Cover the Dutch oven or casserole and bake for 3 to 4 hours, or until the venison is quite tender.
5. Enjoy!

27.Slow Cooker Rabbit Stew With Sour Cream

Ingredients

- 2 rabbits, cleaned and cut up
- 1/2 teaspoon kosher salt
- 1/4 teaspoon freshly ground black pepper
- 1/2 teaspoon paprika
- 2 small carrots, sliced
- 1/2 cup chopped onion
- 6 ounces canned sliced mushrooms, drained
- 2 sprigs of rosemary (or thyme)
- 10 3/4 ounces cream of mushroom soup, undiluted
- 1/4 teaspoon Worcestershire sauce
- 1 cup sour cream

Instructions

1. Sprinkle the meat with salt, pepper, and paprika and arrange it in the bowl of a slow cooker. Layer the carrots and onions on top of the meat, along with the mushrooms, if using.
2. Add a few sprigs of fresh rosemary or thyme to the mixture.
3. In a bowl, combine the condensed soup with the Worcestershire sauce. Stir the mixture and spoon it over the meat.
4. Cover and cook on low for 5 to 6 hours, or until the meat is tender and thoroughly cooked. According to the USDA, the minimum safe temperature for rabbit is 160 F.
5. Add the sour cream, stir gently to blend, and cook for about 20 to 30 minutes longer, or until hot.
6. Serve the stew with crusty bread or biscuits and a tossed salad.

28.Hearty Rabbit Stew With Vegetables Recipe

Ingredients

- **For the Stew**
- 1 rabbit (about 3 pounds, cut up)
- 3/4 cup all-purpose flour (divided)
- 3 tablespoons butter
- 1 cup celery (chopped)
- 2 medium onions (thinly sliced)
- 1 teaspoon seasoned salt
- 1 teaspoon salt
- Dash of pepper
- 1 bay leaf
- 4 cups water (or a low-sodium vegetable or chicken broth)
- 4 cups dry red wine
- 2 cups diced carrots
- 4 medium potatoes (peeled and diced)
- 4 ounces sliced mushrooms (sautéed)
- 1/3 cup water (cold)
- **For the Optional Sage Dumplings**
- 2 cups of biscuit mix
- 3/4 cup of milk
- 1/2 teaspoon poultry seasoning

Instructions

Note: while there are multiple steps to this recipe, this stew is broken down into workable categories to help you better plan for preparation and cooking.

Make the Rabbit Stew

1. Gather the ingredients.
2. Dredge the rabbit pieces with the 1/2 cup of flour.
3. Melt butter in a Dutch oven over medium heat; brown rabbit pieces on all sides.
4. Add celery, onion, seasoned salt, salt, pepper, bay leaf, 4 cups water or broth, and wine; bring to a boil.
5. Reduce heat to a simmer, cover, and simmer for 2 hours.
6. Add carrots, potatoes, and mushrooms. Cook for about 25 to 30 minutes longer, or until vegetables are tender.
7. In a small bowl, combine remaining 1/4 cup flour and 1/3 cup of cold water; stir until well blended and free of lumps.

8. Stir the flour mixture into the broth; cook and stir until the broth has thickened.
9. Serve the stew with biscuits and a salad.

Optional Sage Dumplings

1. Gather the ingredients.
2. If you're making the optional sage dumplings, after thickening the stew, combine 2 cups of biscuit mix in a bowl with 3/4 cup of milk and 1/2 teaspoon of poultry seasoning. Stir with a fork until the ingredients are combined.
3. Drop over the simmering stew and cook for 10 minutes.
4. Cover the pan and continue simmering for 10 minutes longer, gently stirring occasionally to keep the stew from scorching.
5. Serve and enjoy!

29.Crock Pot Lamb Stew

Ingredients

- 2 1/2 cups chicken stock (low sodium or unsalted)
- 1 1/2 tablespoons olive oil (extra-virgin)
- 2 pounds lamb
- 3 medium carrots
- 2 medium onions
- 1 pound red-skinned (or round white potatoes)
- 1/4 teaspoon Kosher salt
- 1/8 teaspoon black pepper (freshly ground)
- 2 tablespoons flour
- 3 tablespoons water (cold)
- Optional: 1 to 2 tablespoons parsley (chopped)

Instructions

1. Gather the ingredients.
2. Cut the lamb into bite-size pieces.
3. Heat the oil in a large skillet over medium-high heat. When the oil is hot and simmering, add the lamb and cook until all sides are well-browned.
4. Meanwhile, peel and thinly slice the carrots. Peel the potatoes and slice or dice them. Peel the onions, cut into quarters, and slice thinly.
5. Put the carrots, onions, and potatoes in the slow cooker. Arrange the browned lamb pieces on the vegetables.

6. Pour the chicken stock into the skillet used to cook the lamb. Bring the stock to a boil, stirring to get all of the browned bits. Taste and add salt and pepper, as needed.
7. Add the hot chicken broth to the crock pot.
8. Cover and cook for 3 to 4 hours on high or 6 to 8 hours on low.
9. In a small bowl or cup, combine the 2 tablespoons of flour with the 3 tablespoons of cold water. Whisk until the mixture is smooth with no lumps.
10. Stir the slurry into the stew mixture and continue cooking for about 10 to 15 minutes.
11. Sprinkle fresh chopped parsley over the stew and serve it hot with thick, crusty bread. Irish soda bread is also a good choice, or make homemade bread or biscuits.

12. Enjoy!

30.Classic Irish Stew With Lamb

Ingredients

- 1 tablespoon extra-virgin olive oil
- 1 1/2 to 2 pounds lamb shoulder (trimmed and cut into 1-inch pieces)
- 2 to 3 medium onions (quartered and sliced)
- 1 teaspoon dried leaf thyme
- 1 1/2 cups carrots (diced or sliced peeled)
- 1 large bay leaf
- 3 cups chicken stock (or broth)
- 1 1/2 pounds potatoes (cut into 1-inch chunks)
- Salt (to taste)
- Freshly ground black pepper (to taste)
- Optional: 2 tablespoons fresh chopped parsley
- 2 tablespoons all-purpose flour

Directions

1. In a large, deep sauté pan or Dutch oven over medium-high heat, sauté the lamb in the oil, stirring, for 2 minutes.
2. Add the onion and continue cooking, stirring, until the lamb is browned and onion is tender, about 3 to 5 minutes.

3. Sprinkle with thyme and add the carrots, bay leaf, and stock. Bring to a simmer; reduce heat to low, cover, and simmer for about 1 hour.
4. Add the potatoes to the pan, cover, and continue cooking for 25 minutes. Taste and add salt and pepper, as desired. Stir the chopped parsley into the stew, if using.
5. In a cup or bowl, stir flour into the cold water until the mixture is smooth. Add to the stew, stir well, and cook for a minute or two, until thickened.
6. Serve the lamb stew with a salad and crusty rolls for a delicious meal.

31. Traditional Slow Cooker Irish Lamb Stew

Ingredients

- 2 1/2 pounds boneless lamb (cut into 1 1/2-inch cubes)
- 2 tablespoons vegetable oil
- 1 1/2 teaspoons salt
- 1/2 teaspoon pepper
- 4 turnips (or one medium rutabaga)
- 4 carrots
- 2 medium onions
- 4 medium red-skinned potatoes
- 2 cups water or unsalted stock
- 2 tablespoons all-purpose flour
- 2 tablespoons chopped parsley

Directions

1. Heat the vegetable oil in a large skillet over medium-high heat. Add the lamb cubes and cook, turning frequently to brown all sides.
2. Meanwhile, prepare the vegetables. Cut the turnips into 1/2-inch cubes. Peel the carrot and slice it into 1/2-inch thick rounds. Peel the onion and chop it coarsely. Quarter the potatoes (peel if desired.)
3. Add the lamb to the slow cooker along with the salt, pepper, turnip, carrots, onions, and potatoes. Add 2 cups of water or stock. If you use regular stock or broth with salt, don't add until the end of the cooking time.
4. Add 2 cups water and cook on low, covered, for 8 to 10 hours. Uncover and turn on high. Blend flour with 1/4 cup water until it forms a paste; slowly add it to the stew, stirring constantly until slightly thickened. Stir in parsley, and serve.

32.Spiced Lamb Stew

Ingredients

- 1 1/2 to 2 pounds boneless lamb shoulder (or stewing lamb)
- 1/2 teaspoon kosher salt (or to taste)
- 1/4 teaspoon ground black pepper
- 1/4 cup all-purpose flour
- 1 tablespoon olive oil
- 1 medium onion (chopped)
- 2 cloves garlic (minced)
- 1/2 teaspoon ground cumin
- 1/2 teaspoon ground ginger
- 1/4 teaspoon ground cinnamon
- dash coarsely ground black pepper
- 1 medium carrot (peeled, diced)
- 1 (14.5-ounce) can tomatoes (with juice, diced)
- 1 cup chicken stock
- Juice of 1/2 lemon

Directions

1. Trim any visible fat from the lamb and cut it into bite-size pieces. Sprinkle with salt and pepper and then toss with the flour.
2. Heat 1 tablespoon of olive oil—or vegetable oil—in a Dutch oven or large saucepan over medium heat. Add the floured lamb pieces and the chopped onion. Cook the lamb until browned on all sides, stirring frequently.
3. Add the onion and cook, stirring, for about 5 minutes longer, or until the onion is translucent.
4. Add the garlic and cook, stirring, for 1 minute longer.
5. Add remaining ingredients and bring to a boil.
6. Reduce heat, cover, and simmer for about 1 hour, until lamb is tender.
7. Serve over hot cooked rice, grits or polenta, or couscous, or serve with hot buttered noodles or potatoes.

33.Lamb Stew With Parsley Dumplings

Ingredients

- 2 tablespoons shortening or cooking oil
- 2 pounds cubed lean lamb shoulder
- 4 cups water
- 2 teaspoons salt
- 1/4 teaspoon pepper
- 1 bay leaf
- 3 carrots, cut into 1-inch slices
- 2 small to medium potatoes, peeled and cut into 1-inch chunks
- 1 medium onion, halved and sliced
- 1 cup frozen green peas, thawed
- 2 tablespoons flour
- 3 tablespoons cold water
- **Parsley Dumplings:**
- 2 cups biscuit mix
- 3/4 cup milk
- 1 teaspoon dried parsley flakes or 1 tablespoon minced fresh parsley

Directions

1. Melt shortening or oil in a Dutch oven; brown lamb cubes well; pour off fat. To the lamb, add the 4 cups water, salt and pepper, and bay leaf. Bring to a boil then reduce heat; cover and simmer for 2 hours, until meat is tender.
2. Stir in carrots, onion, and potato; cook 20 minutes longer. Stir in the thawed peas.
3. Blend 2 tablespoons flour with the 3 tablespoons water; Stir into stew. Cook until mixture begins to boil and thicken.
4. Mix dumpling ingredients with a fork until well moistened, but do not overmix. Spoon dumplings onto gently boiling stew, trying to keep the dumplings on the meat and vegetables and not too far into the liquid.
5. Cook slowly over low heat for 10 minutes, uncovered.
6. Cover and cook 10 minutes longer over low heat. Dumplings will have a biscuit-like texture inside when done.
7. Check the stew for scorching while they cook, but be careful not to break up the dumplings.

34.Lamb Stew With Herb Dumplings

Ingredients

- 3 tablespoons vegetable oil
- 2 pounds lamb stew meat (or stew beef)
- 1/2 cup flour
- 1 1/2 cups onion (chopped)
- 2 carrots (chopped into large pieces)
- 4 potatoes (diced)
- 2 tomatoes (peeled and chopped, or 1 (14.5-ounce) can diced tomatoes)
- 1/2 teaspoon garlic powder
- 1 bunch fresh mixed herbs tied with a string (thyme, rosemary, chives, parsley)
- 2 1/2 cups beef broth
- **Herb Dumplings:**
- 2 cups biscuit baking mix
- 2/3 cup milk
- 1/2 to 1 teaspoon mixed dried herbs or parsley

Directions

1. Put the vegetable oil in a large, heavy skillet and place it over medium-high heat.
2. Coat meat in flour and then brown in oil in a skillet.
3. Add onions and cook until lightly browned.
4. Place the browned meat, onions and vegetables in a large stockpot or Dutch oven. Add garlic powder. Place the bundle of herbs in the middle of the mixture. Cover with the beef broth and simmer for 2 hours over low heat.
5. While stew is cooking, make dumplings (see below). Salt and pepper to taste.
6. About 20 minutes before serving time, combine the biscuit baking mix with the milk and dried herbs or parsley. Mix until moistened.
7. Drop onto the boiling stew and simmer gently for 10 minutes.
8. Cover the pan and continue simmering for 10 minutes longer.
9. Serve and enjoy!

35.Instant Pot Chicken and Dumplings

Ingredients

- **For the Dumplings:**
- 1 1/2 cups all-purpose flour
- 3/4 teaspoon salt
- 2 1/2 teaspoons baking powder
- 3 tablespoons unsalted butter (melted)
- 3/4 cup milk
- **For the Stew:**
- 2 tablespoons olive oil
- 1 onion (diced, about 3/4 cup)
- 3 cloves garlic (minced, about 1 tablespoon)
- 4 cups chicken stock (low sodium or unsalted)
- 1 teaspoon kosher salt (or to taste)
- 1/4 teaspoon black pepper
- 1 teaspoon poultry seasoning
- 2 carrots (diced, about 1 cup)
- 3 stalks celery (diced, about 1 cup)
- 1 1/2 pounds chicken breasts (cut into 1-inch cubes)
- 1 cup frozen peas (thawed)
- 3 tablespoons parsley (fresh, chopped, plus more for garnish)
- 1/2 cup heavy cream

Directions

1. Gather the ingredients.
2. In a medium mixing bowl, combine the flour, 3/4 teaspoon of salt, the baking powder, and melted butter. Add the milk and stir to form a soft dough. Set aside.
3. Select the sauté function on the Instant Pot and heat the olive oil. When the olive oil is hot, add the diced onion. Cook, stirring, for 2 minutes. Add the minced garlic and cook for about 1 minute longer. Cancel the sauté function.
4. Add the chicken stock to the pot and stir, scraping up any browned bits that may be on the bottom of the pot. Stir in the salt, pepper, and poultry seasoning, and then add the carrots, celery, and cubed chicken.
5. Scoop the dumpling dough up with a cookie scoop or tablespoon, allowing about 2 tablespoons for each dumpling. Place the dumplings atop the stew mixture.
6. Lock the lid in place and move the steam release vent to the sealing position. Select the pressure cook setting (or manual on older models), high pressure, and set the time for 8 minutes. When the time is up, allow a natural release for 15

minutes and then carefully move the steam release vent to the venting position to release the remaining steam.

7. Carefully remove the dumplings to a bowl and cover with foil to keep warm. Add the peas and all but a few pinches of the parsley to the stew. Select the sauté function and cook for 2 to 3 minutes, or just until the peas are tender. Stir the heavy cream into the stew and heat through. Taste and adjust the seasonings.
8. Ladle the stew into bowls and top with one or two dumplings. Sprinkle servings with some of the remaining chopped parsley.
9. Enjoy!

36.Crock Pot Oxtail Stew

Ingredients

- 3 tablespoons extra virgin olive oil
- 3 to 4 lbs. oxtails (disjointed)
- 2 medium onions (chopped)
- 2 cloves garlic, finely chopped
- 1 tablespoon all-purpose flour
- 2 potatoes (cut in chunks)
- 2 carrots (chopped)
- 1 1/2 cups beef stock
- 3/4 cup dry red wine
- 1/2 cup tomato sauce
- 6 peppercorns
- 1/2 teaspoon dried oregano
- 1 dried red chile pepper (seeded and chopped)
- 2 whole cloves
- 1 red bell pepper (chopped)
- 1 tablespoon parsley (chopped)

Directions

1. Gather the ingredients.
2. Heat the oil in a large skillet over medium-high heat; brown the oxtails on all sides.
3. Reduce the heat to medium; add the onions and cook for 5 minutes longer.
4. Add the garlic and cook for 1 minute longer.
5. Sprinkle the flour over the meat and vegetables and stir to blend. Cook for 2 minutes longer.

6. Put potatoes in bottom of the crock pot along with carrots.
7. Add the oxtail mixture.
8. Deglaze the pan with the red wine and pour over the oxtails in the slow cooker.
9. Add the beef broth to the slow cooker along with the tomato sauce, peppercorns, oregano, chile pepper, cloves, bell pepper, and parsley. Add salt and pepper, to taste.

10. Cover and cook on low for 9 to 11 hours, or until the oxtails are very tender.
11. Serve and enjoy!

37. Jamaican-Style Oxtail Stew

Ingredients

- 1/3 cup small white beans (dried)
- 2 cups water (approximately, divided)
- 3 pounds beef oxtails
- 1 tablespoon lard (freshly rendered or vegetable oil)
- 3 cloves garlic (peeled and crushed)
- 1 medium onion (yellow, peeled, and diced)
- 1 medium tomato (diced)
- 2 cups beef stock (homemade or canned)
- 2 tablespoons allspice (freshly ground or to taste)
- Salt (to taste)
- Freshly ground black pepper (to taste)
- Tabasco (to taste)

Directions

1. Gather the ingredients.
2. Place the beans in a small saucepan and add 1 cup of the water.
3. Bring to a boil, covered, and turn off the heat. Allow to sit for 1 hour, covered.
4. Then drain.
5. Brown the oxtails well in the lard or oil.
6. Place the oxtails in a 6-quart stovetop casserole, along with the garlic, onion, and tomato. Add the beef stock and enough water so that it just covers the contents of the pot. Then add the allspice, salt, and pepper.
7. Cover and simmer for 1 1/2 hours, then add the drained beans.

8. Simmer for an additional 2 hours, stirring occasionally. Remove the lid during the last hour of cooking if you prefer a thicker sauce. Be careful that the pot does not boil dry; if it looks imminent, add a bit more water.
9. Taste and add more salt and pepper, if needed, and a few shots of Tabasco, to taste.
10. Enjoy!

38.Oxtail Stew in Red Wine Recipe

Ingredients

- 2 3/4 pounds oxtails
- Salt and pepper (to taste)
- 1/4 cup olive oil
- 2 cups chopped onion
- 1 1/2 cups chopped leeks (white and light green parts)
- 1 teaspoon minced garlic
- 1/2 cup diced plum tomatoes
- 1 tablespoon sherry vinegar (or to taste)
- 1 tablespoon honey
- 2 cups dry red wine
- 3 cups beef broth
- 4 fresh parsley sprigs
- 4 fresh thyme sprigs
- 1 bay leaf

Directions

1. Generously season oxtails with salt and pepper. In a large Dutch oven or casserole, heat oil on high heat until it shimmers. Add oxtails in a single layer to hot oil, working in batches if necessary, and sear the oxtails until browned on all sides, about 10 minutes. Remove oxtails with tongs to a plate (leaving the oil behind). Cover oxtails loosely and set aside.
2. Return Dutch oven to high heat until oil shimmers. Add onion, leeks, and garlic and saute, stirring occasionally, until golden brown, about 15 minutes. Add tomatoes and cook until it deepens in color and smells sweet about 2 minutes.
3. Add sherry vinegar and honey. Stir until honey is dissolved. Return oxtails and any juices to the Dutch oven, stirring gently with a wooden spoon. Add red wine and enough broth to cover. Bring to a boil, reduce heat and add a bouquet garni made by tying the parsley, thyme and bay leaf together in cheesecloth with

butcher's twine. Cover and let simmer over very low heat until meat is nearly falling off the bone, about 2 to 3 hours.

4. Transfer oxtails to a heated serving bowl and keep warm. Remove and discard the bouquet garni. Return Dutch oven to heat. Skim off fat and oil from the surface of pan juices and bring to a simmer over medium-high heat, until juices have thickened slightly about 5 minutes. Season to taste with sherry vinegar, salt, and pepper. Pour sauce over oxtail pieces and serve immediately with roasted potatoes or mamaliga.

39.Hungarian Tomato-Pepper Stew (Lecso)

Ingredients

- 2 tablespoons bacon grease (or oil)
- 1 medium onion (sliced thinly)
- 1 pound peppers (Hungarian wax, banana, Italian or green bell peppers, cut into 1/4-inch strips)
- 3 large very ripe tomatoes (peeled and chopped, or use the shortcut above)
- 1 1/2 teaspoons sugar
- 1 1/2 teaspoons salt (less if using sausage)
- 1 tablespoon sweet Hungarian paprika

Directions

1. Gather the ingredients.
2. In a large skillet, sauté the onion in bacon fat or oil over low heat for 5 minutes.
3. Add pepper strips and cook another 15 minutes.
4. Add tomatoes, sugar, salt, and paprika and cook for another 25 to 30 minutes, stirring occasionally, or until mixture resembles chunky tomato sauce.

40.Sambar: Indian Vegetable Stew

Ingredients

- 2 cups Toor or Tuvar (split yellow pigeon peas)
- 4 tablespoons Sambar Masala
- 1 cup chopped eggplant (cut into 2"cubes)
- 1 cup chopped potato (cut into 1"cubes)
- 10 pearl onions, peeled and cored
- 10-12 baby okra
- 1/2 cup pumpkin
- 10-12, 3" long pieces of drumstick (optional)
- Golf ball-sized lump of tamarind
- 3 tablespoons ghee (clarified butter)
- 1 teaspoon mustard seeds
- 8-10 curry leaves
- 3 dry red chilies
- Salt to taste
- Chopped fresh coriander leaves to taste

Directions

1. Boil the lentils and Sambar Masala with enough water till they are soft. The consistency should be that of a thick soup.
2. Soak the tamarind in a small bowl of hot water for 10 minutes. Squeeze well to remove all juice.
3. Add this purée to the lentils. Mix well. Add salt to taste.
4. Simmer and add the potatoes to the lentils. Cook until the potatoes are half cooked. Now add the other vegetables and cook until done.
5. Heat the ghee in a small pan and add the dry red chilies, mustard seeds, and curry leaves. Fry until the spluttering stops and add to the boiled lentils. Mix well.
6. Garnish with chopped green coriander and serve hot with Idlis, Vadas or plain boiled rice.

41.Polish Hunter's Stew (Bigos) Recipe

Ingredients

- 1 cup prunes (pitted)
- 1/2 ounce Polish *borowiki* mushrooms (dried or dried Italian porcini mushrooms)
- 2 cups water (boiling)
- 1 tablespoon bacon fat (or vegetable oil)
- 1 medium onion (chopped)
- 1 small head cabbage (chopped)
- 1 pound sauerkraut (rinsed well and drained)
- 1/2 pound smoked Polish sausage (cut into 1-inch pieces)
- 1/2 pound fresh Polish sausage (cooked and cut into 1-inch pieces)
- 1 pound meat leftovers (any type, boneless, cut into 1-inch pieces)
- 3 large tomatoes (peeled and chopped)
- 1 cup dry red wine (preferably Madeira)
- 1 bay leaf
- 1 teaspoon salt (or to taste)
- 1/4 teaspoon pepper (or to taste)

Directions

1. Gather the ingredients.
2. Place prunes and dried mushrooms in a medium heatproof bowl. Pour 2 cups boiling water over the prunes and mushrooms and let them steep for 30 minutes or until the mushrooms have softened. You can chop the mushrooms and prunes if you wish, but leaving them whole makes for a chunkier dish. Set aside with soaking liquid.
3. Meanwhile, in a Dutch oven or a large pot with a lid, sauté onion and fresh cabbage in bacon drippings or vegetable oil.
4. When cabbage has collapsed by half, add the sauerkraut, sausages, leftover meat, tomatoes, wine, bay leaf, and reserved mushrooms and prunes and their soaking liquid. Be careful not to include the sandy sediment in the bottom of the soaking bowl.
5. Mix well and bring to a boil over medium heat.
6. Turn heat to low and simmer covered for 1 1/2 hours, stirring occasionally and adding liquid as necessary to prevent burning.

7. When ready to serve, remove bay leaf. Portion into heated bowls and garnish with

   a piece of frisée or other fancy greens to resemble the feather in a hunter's hat.
8. Enjoy!

42.Oxtail Stew in Red Wine

Ingredients

- 2 3/4 pounds oxtails
- Salt and pepper (to taste)
- 1/4 cup olive oil
- 2 cups chopped onion
- 1 1/2 cups chopped leeks (white and light green parts)
- 1 teaspoon minced garlic
- 1/2 cup diced plum tomatoes
- 1 tablespoon sherry vinegar (or to taste)
- 1 tablespoon honey
- 2 cups dry red wine
- 3 cups beef broth
- 4 fresh parsley sprigs
- 4 fresh thyme sprigs
- 1 bay leaf

Directions

1. Generously season oxtails with salt and pepper. In a large Dutch oven or casserole, heat oil on high heat until it shimmers. Add oxtails in a single layer to hot oil, working in batches if necessary, and sear the oxtails until browned on all sides, about 10 minutes. Remove oxtails with tongs to a plate (leaving the oil behind). Cover oxtails loosely and set aside.
2. Return Dutch oven to high heat until oil shimmers. Add onion, leeks, and garlic and saute, stirring occasionally, until golden brown, about 15 minutes. Add tomatoes and cook until it deepens in color and smells sweet about 2 minutes.
3. Add sherry vinegar and honey. Stir until honey is dissolved. Return oxtails and any juices to the Dutch oven, stirring gently with a wooden spoon. Add red wine and enough broth to cover. Bring to a boil, reduce heat and add a bouquet garni made by tying the parsley, thyme and bay leaf together in cheesecloth with

butcher's twine. Cover and let simmer over very low heat until meat is nearly falling off the bone, about 2 to 3 hours.

4. Transfer oxtails to a heated serving bowl and keep warm. Remove and discard the bouquet garni. Return Dutch oven to heat. Skim off fat and oil from the surface of pan juices and bring to a simmer over medium-high heat, until juices have thickened slightly about 5 minutes. Season to taste with sherry vinegar, salt, and pepper. Pour sauce over oxtail pieces and serve immediately with roasted potatoes or mamaliga.

43.Russian Root Vegetable Stew

Ingredients

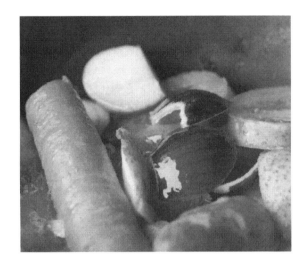

- 1 tablespoon sunflower or vegetable oil
- 1 large onion (finely chopped)
- 4 carrots (peeled and cut into 2-inch lengths)
- 2 large red potatoes (peeled and cut into 2-inch pieces)
- 1 medium rutabaga (peeled and cut into 2-inch pieces)
- 1 medium turnip (peeled and cut into 2-inch pieces)
- 1 parsnip (peeled and cut into 2-inch lengths)
- 1 medium celeriac (celery root, peeled and cut into 2-inch pieces)
- 1 cup vegetable stock
- 1/2 cup parsley (finely chopped)
- 2 tablespoons butter

Directions

1. In a large skillet or Dutch oven, saute onion in oil over medium heat until translucent, about 3 to 5 minutes.
2. Add the carrots, potatoes, rutabaga, turnip, parsnip, and celeriac, and saute, stirring frequently, for about 10 minutes or until vegetables begin to collapse.
3. Add stock, bring to a boil, cover, reduce heat and simmer for 20 minutes until vegetables are soft but still hold their shape.
4. Add parsley and butter and stir until butter has melted. Season to taste with salt and pepper.
5. Serve with dark rye bread or sourdough rye bread and butter.

6. Enjoy!

44.Easy Croatian Shrimp

Ingredients

- 3 pounds head-on large shrimp (or 1 1/2 pounds tail-on, peeled large shrimp)
- 1/2 cup olive oil
- 1/4 cup fresh breadcrumbs
- 1 tablespoon garlic (minced, or to taste)
- 1/4 cup fresh parsley (finely chopped)
- 1 (14-ounce) can peeled whole tomatoes (undrained and broken up)
- 1 teaspoon Vegeta seasoning (see note below)
- 2 cups dry white wine
- Salt (to taste)
- Pepper (to taste)

Steps to Make It

1. Gather the ingredients.
2. De-vein, rinse, and pat dry the head-on or tail-on shrimp and set aside.
3. Heat a large skillet with a lid over medium heat. Add the oil followed by the breadcrumbs and stir. Cook, uncovered, just until the breadcrumbs turn golden and smell toasty.
4. Add the garlic, parsley, tomatoes, and Vegeta seasoning. Bring to a boil. Reduce the heat and simmer, uncovered, for 10 minutes.
5. Add the wine, season with salt and pepper, and bring to a boil. Add the shrimp, reduce the heat, and cover with the lid. Simmer 15 to 20 minutes or until shrimp are cooked through and the juices have thickened. Don't overcook or the shrimp will become rubbery.
6. Remove the shrimp from the skillet with tongs and place in a large bowl. Pour the cooking juices into a gravy boat or similar container.
7. Place everything on the table, letting guests peel the shrimp at their place settings and pour their own sauce. Serve with polenta, cornbread, or crusty bread that can be dipped into the flavorful sauce.

45.Easy Hungarian Goulash

Ingredients

- 2 to 3 pounds boneless chuck roast (cut into 1-inch chunks)
- Kosher salt
- Freshly ground black pepper
- 2 tablespoons all-purpose flour
- 3 tablespoons olive oil (divided)
- 4 medium sweet onions (sliced and separated into rings)
- 8 ounces baby portobello mushrooms (or cremini mushrooms, brushed clean and cut in half)
- 1 head garlic (about 12 cloves, peeled, large cloves cut in half)
- 1/2 cup sweet red wine
- 1 3/4 cups beef broth
- 1 (4-ounce) jar diced roasted red peppers
- 1/4 cup sweet Hungarian paprika
- 1 cup sour cream
- 4 cups cooked buttered noodles
- A handful of chopped fresh parsley

Directions

1. Gather the ingredients.
2. Place beef chunks in a large bowl. Sprinkle liberally with salt and pepper and toss with the flour.
3. Heat a heavy Dutch oven over medium-high heat and add 1 tablespoon of the olive oil. Swirl to coat the bottom of the pan.
4. Place beef chunks in a single layer and brown on two sides. (You will probably need to do this in batches; do not crowd the meat or it will boil instead of brown.)
5. Remove browned beef to a bowl.
6. Reduce heat to medium-low. To the drippings in the Dutch oven, add the remaining 2 tablespoons of olive oil, onion rings, mushrooms, and garlic. Toss to coat with the olive oil.
7. Cover tightly and sweat the vegetables, stirring occasionally, until onions are limp but not browned and mushrooms are releasing their liquid, about 10 minutes.
8. Add red wine to the vegetables and cook 2 minutes, scraping up browned bits from the bottom.

9. Add beef broth, roasted red peppers, and paprika.
10. Return beef and any accumulated juices to the pan. Stir until well-combined.
11. Cover tightly, reduce heat, and simmer on low heat for 1 1/2 to 2 hours, stirring occasionally, until beef is fork-tender.
12. Remove Dutch oven from heat and wait for boiling to subside. Taste and add additional salt if necessary. Stir in sour cream until completely incorporated into the gravy.

13. Serve Hungarian goulash over hot buttered noodles with chopped parsley.
14. Enjoy!

46. Croatian Bean Soup

Ingredients

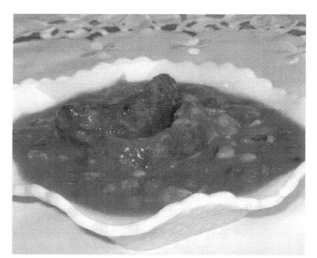

- 1 pound dried beans (rinsed, picked over, and soaked overnight)
- 12 to 15 cups cold water
- 3 cloves garlic (peeled and minced)
- 1 large onion (chopped)
- 1 pound smoked sausage (Croatian, like *kranjska, kobasice,* or smoked Polish sausage like *kiełbasa krajana,* cut into 4-inch lengths)
- 1 pound smoked ribs (or meaty smoked ham hocks)
- 1 large bay leaf
- Salt, pepper, and Vegeta to taste

Directions

1. Rinse the beans and pick them over to remove shriveled beans, bits of rock, and any other matter that doesn't belong there. Place in a large bowl or pot and add cool water to come about 3 inches above the beans. Cover and soak overnight at room temperature. Alternatively, use the quick soak method.
2. When you are ready to prepare this recipe, drain the beans, rinse them, and drain again. Place in a large pot and add 12 cups fresh cold water. Bring to a boil, reduce heat to a simmer, and skim off any foam that rises to the surface.
3. Add garlic, onion, smoked sausage of choice, smoked ribs or meaty smoked ham hocks, bay leaf, salt, pepper and Vegeta seasoning powder to taste.

4. Return to a boil, reduce heat, and simmer, partially covered, for 2 to 3 hours or until beans and meat are tender. Add water as needed, while cooking, stirring occasionally.
5. Remove bay leaf and discard. Remove bones from rib meat or hocks and return meat to the pot. If soup isn't thick enough, continue to simmer until desired consistency is achieved.
6. Serve in heated bowls with hearty bread and a glass of beer.

47.Myrna's Hungarian Chicken Paprikash

Ingredients

- 3 1/2 pounds chicken pieces (skin on, rinsed and patted dry)
- 1 tsp. salt
- 1/4 tsp. pepper
- 3 tablespoons rendered chicken fat (shmaltz, see below; or vegetable oil)
- 1 medium onion (chopped)
- 6 to 8 cups water (or enough to almost cover chicken)
- 2 teaspoons sweet Hungarian paprika
- 2 cups rice (long-grain, soaked in cold water 30 minutes and drained)
- 4 cups hot liquid (water from the simmered chicken plus chicken broth)

Directions

1. Generously season both sides of chicken pieces with salt and pepper and let sit while you saute the onions.
2. In a large lidded skillet, heat shmaltz or oil, and saute onions until light golden brown. Remove from skillet and place in a lidded casserole dish or Dutch oven.
3. Brown chicken pieces on all sides in same skillet onion was sauteed in. Move some chicken pieces aside and add the paprika and cook 30 seconds to toast it slightly. Then add water to almost cover the chicken, mixing in with the paprika. Cover and simmer on low for 1 hour.
4. Heat oven to 350 degrees. Place soaked, rinsed and drained rice in the same casserole dish or Dutch oven as sauteed onions. Measure the liquid from the simmering chicken and add chicken broth to make 4 cups of liquid. Pour over the rice, mixing well.
   Place cooked chicken on top of the rice, cover and bake 30 minutes. Uncover

casserole or Dutch oven and cook another 5 minutes. Serve hot with a green vegetable.

48.Croatian Venison Goulash

Ingredients

- 5 pounds venison roast from the hindquarters, cubed into 1-inch squares
- 2 large chopped white onions
- 4 finely chopped garlic cloves
- 1/4 cup olive oil
- 1 large bay leaf
- 4 cups chicken stock or water
- 4 tablespoons sweet Hungarian paprika
- Salt to taste
- 3 tablespoons Vegeta
- 1/4 cup peeled and sliced carrots (optional)
- 1/4 cup sliced mushrooms (optional)
- 1/2 teaspoon black pepper
- 1/4 teaspoon cayenne pepper

Directions

1. Place venison cubes in a nonmetallic container and rub them with onions, garlic, olive oil, and bay leaf, cover with plastic wrap and marinate overnight.
2. Remove bay leaf and sear meat on medium-high heat in batches using a large earthenware pot or large stock pot. There should be enough oil from marinating so meat doesn't stick.
3. Return all seared meat and any exuded juices to the pot, and add stock or water. Bring to a boil, reduce heat and simmer on low, covered, for approximately 3 hours, stirring frequently, adding more stock or water, if necessary.
4. Add paprika and salt. Continue to cook for another hour or until the meat is tender and falling apart. Add the Vegeta, carrots and mushrooms, if using, and black and cayenne peppers.
5. Continue cooking until meat and vegetables are very tender. Serve over polenta, mamaliga, mashed potatoes or noodles.

49.Slow-Cooker Cowboy Stew With Beef and Beans

Ingredients

- 1 tablespoon canola or vegetable oil
- 1 cup chopped onion
- 1 pound lean ground beef or ground chuck
- 1 can (15 ounces) prepared chili beans
- 1 can (15 ounces) pork and beans
- 1 can (12 to 15 ounces) cream-style corn
- 1 can (15 ounces) tomato sauce
- Optional: 1 green or red bell pepper, chopped
- Garnish: sour cream, shredded cheese, chopped avocado

Directions

1. Heat the oil in a large skillet over medium-high heat until it begins to shimmer.
2. Add the onion and bell pepper, if desired. Sauté for 5 minutes or until the vegetables start to soften.
3. Add the ground beef and cook, stirring often and breaking up any large clumps of meat, until no pink remains. Drain well.
4. Combine the beef mixture in the slow cooker with the beans, cream-style corn, and tomato sauce; cover and cook on low for 5 to 8 hours.

50.Crockpot Beef and Beer Stew

Ingredients

- 2 1/2 pounds lean beef stew meat (cut into 1-inch cubes)
- 1 large onion (chopped)
- 2 cloves garlic (minced)
- 3 carrots (cut into 1-inch slices)
- 2 ribs celery (cut into 1/2-inch slices)
- 2 medium potatoes (cut into 1-inch cubes)

- 1 cup beer
- 1 cup beef broth (or use all beer and no beef broth)
- 1 1/2 teaspoon salt
- 1/2 teaspoon pepper
- 1 teaspoon oregano
- 2 tablespoons tomato paste
- 3 tablespoon melted butter
- 1/3 cup all-purpose flour

Directions

1. Gather the ingredients.
2. In the slow cooker crockery insert, combine the stew beef, onion, garlic, carrots, celery, potatoes, beer, beef broth, salt, pepper, oregano, and tomato paste.
3. Cover and cook on LOW for 8 to 10 hours.
4. Mix melted butter with flour until a smooth mixture forms.
5. Add this to the stew to thicken it. Taste and adjust seasonings.
6. Turn the slow cooker to HIGH and cook until the desired thickness is reached, about 15 to 20 minutes.
7. Serve right away and enjoy.

51.Slow Cooker Barbecue Beer Beef Stew

Ingredients

- Kosher salt and freshly ground pepper to taste
- 1 teaspoon garlic powder
- 2 teaspoons olive or vegetable oil
- 3 pounds beef stew meat, cut into 1-inch cubes
- 1½ cups chopped onion
- 1 cup barbecue sauce, homemade or store-bought
- 1 cup beef broth
- 2 tablespoons honey
- 1 tablespoon Dijon mustard
- 2 cups ½-inch pieces peeled or scrubbed parsnips
- ¾ cup beer
- 1 pound egg noodles

Directions

1. Gather the ingredients.
2. Season the beef evenly with salt, pepper, and the garlic powder.
3. Heat the oil in a large pan over medium high heat. Working in batches, brown the meat until it is browned on all sides, about 10 minutes for each batch. Don't crowd the beef cubes in the pan. Set the meat aside.
4. Pour off all but 2 teaspoons of fat from the pan and add the onions. Sauté them for 3 minutes, until lightly browned, and add them to the slow cooker. In the slow cooker, mix together the barbecue sauce, beef broth, honey and mustard. Add the parsnips, browned beef and the cooked onions to the slow cooker and stir to combine.
5. Add the beer to the slow cooker, and cook on low for 6 to 8 hours, until the meat is tender. When the stew is ready, prepare the egg noodles according to package directions. Serve hot with noodles.

52. Chilean Beef Stew

Ingredients

- 1 pound stewing beef (cut into 1 inch cubes)
- 1 tablespoon flour
- 2 tablespoons butter
- 3 1/2 ounce package of beef jerky
- 2 cups beef stock
- 1 large onion (chopped)
- 2 cloves garlic (minced)
- 2 tablespoons vegetable oil
- 1 tablespoon aji panca chile pepper paste, or minced hot pepper
- 1 acorn squash (peeled, seeded, and cubed)
- 1 cup carrots (chopped)
- 2 large potatoes (peeled and cut into cubes)
- 2/3 cup frozen lima beans
- 2/3 cup frozen corn
- Salt and pepper to taste

Directions

1. Toss the cubes of beef with the flour and season with salt and pepper.

2. Melt the 2 tablespoons of butter in a heavy skillet over medium-high heat. Sauté the cubes of beef until browned.
3. Add the beef stock to the skillet and bring to a simmer over low heat.
4. Chop the beef jerky into small pieces and add to the beef stock and beef cubes. Simmer gently for about 5 minutes.
5. Transfer beef and beef stock to a large stockpot or slow cooker.
6. Do not clean skillet. Add 2 tablespoons vegetable oil, the chopped onion and garlic, and the aji chile pepper paste to the skillet. Sauté until the onion and garlic are soft and fragrant.
7. Add the chopped squash, carrots, and potatoes and sauté for 2-3 minutes.
8. Add sautéed vegetables to the stockpot or crockpot with the beef. Simmer over low heat until beef and beef jerky are tender, about an hour and a half on the stove or about 6 hours in the crockpot. If simmering the stew on the stove, you may need to add more liquid (beef stock or water) from time to time, but stew should finish up very thick, without much broth.
9. Add the lima beans and corn and simmer for 10-15 minutes more.
10. Season with salt and pepper to taste, and serve over rice.

53.Beef Stew With Dumplings

Ingredients

- 2 pounds beef bottom round steak
- 1 bag baby carrots
- 2 stalks celery, chopped
- 2 onions, chopped
- 2 garlic cloves, minced
- 1 (14-ounce) can diced tomatoes, undrained
- 2 cups beef broth
- 1-1/2 teaspoons dried thyme leaves
- 1 teaspoon dried marjoram leaves
- Salt and pepper to taste
- 1/3 cup water
- 3 tablespoons flour
- 1-1/2 cups Bisquick Mix
- 1/2 teaspoon dried thyme leaves
- 1/2 cup milk
- 2 tablespoons butter, melted

Directions

1. Trim excess fat from the steak and cut the beef into 1" pieces. Place in a 4 to 5-quart crockpot along with the carrots, celery, onions, garlic, tomatoes, beef broth, 1-1/2 teaspoons dried thyme, marjoram, salt, and pepper.
2. Cover the slow cooker and cook on low for 8-9 hours until vegetables are tender and the beef is very tender. Then, in a small bowl, combine the water and flour and blend with a wire whisk. Stir this mixture into the crockpot.
3. In a medium bowl, combine the Bisquick Mix (or any purchased baking mix), 1/2 teaspoon thyme, milk, and melted butter just until the dry ingredients are moistened.
4. Drop the dumpling batter by spoonfuls onto the hot and simmering beef mixture in the crockpot. Cover and cook on high for 25 to 35 minutes, until a toothpick poked into the center of the dumplings, comes out clean. Serve immediately.

54. Traditional British Beef Stew and Suet Dumplings

Ingredients

- 2 tablespoons all-purpose flour
- 1 pound/450 grams thick cooking steak (cut into large chunks)
- 2 tablespoons vegetable oil
- 2 tablespoons brandy
- 1 cup/115 grams onion (roughly chopped)
- 1 cup/100 grams leeks (cleaned and finely sliced)
- 1 cup/170 grams carrots (roughly chopped)
- 1 1/2 pints/750 milliliters dark beef stock
- 4 ounces/115 grams self-rising flour
- 2 ounces/55 grams suet (shredded)
- Pinch of salt
- 3 tablespoons water (cold)

Directions

Note: while there are multiple steps to this recipe, this British beef stew, and suet dumplings dish is broken down into workable categories to help you better plan for cooking.

British Beef Stew

1. Gather the ingredients.
2. In a large bowl mix together the flour and the chunks of cooking steak. Make sure all the beef is covered in flour.
3. In a large frying pan heat half the oil to hot but not smoking. Add half the floured steak pieces and brown all over. Remove the steak and place into a Dutch oven or casserole dish. Add the remaining oil to the frying pan, heat again then add the remaining steak and brown all over. Again, add the steak to the dish.
4. Turn the heat up high and add the brandy to the frying pan, stir well, scraping up all the meat juices on the bottom of the pan. Continue to cook this mixture taking care not to burn it until it becomes a sticky glaze.
5. Add the onion, the leeks, and the carrots to the frying pan, stir them well to coat all the vegetables with the glaze, then tip them all into the dish.
6. Place the frying pan back onto the heat; stir in a third of the stock and bring to a boil, scraping all the bits from the bottom of the pan. Once all the bits are released, pour the stock into the casserole.
7. Add the remaining stock, cover with a tight-fitting lid, then simmer gently on the stovetop or in a medium oven (350 F/175 C) for 2 hours. Check from time to time to make sure the stock isn't reducing too much. If it is, add a little boiling water. The meat and vegetables should always be covered by liquid. You can also make this recipe in a slow cooker if you have one.
8. Move on to the next steps for the dumplings.

Suet Dumplings

1. In a roomy bowl, mix the flour with the suet and a pinch of salt. Add 3 tablespoons cold water and stir. If the dough is dry add more water until you have a soft, slightly sticky dough.
2. Divide the dough into 8 pieces and shape into round balls with lightly floured hands. Leave to one side while you roll the remaining dumplings.
3. After the beef stew has cooked for 2 hours, remove the lid, check the seasoning and add salt or pepper to taste. Add the dumplings to the stew, laying them on the surface at even distances apart. Pop one in the middle as well if you have enough. Cover the dish again with the lid and cook for a further 20 minutes.
4. Remove the lid and you will see the dumplings well-risen; if not, cook for a few minutes more.
5. Serve hot into warm bowls.

55.Beef Stew with Newcastle Brown Ale

Ingredients

- 2 pounds plus 3 ounces shin of beef (or use flank or neck, chopped into chunks)
- 3 tablespoons flour
- 3 red onions (peeled, halved and roughly sliced)
- 1 3/4 ounces pancetta (or bacon, chopped)
- 3 sticks celery (chopped)
- 1 small handful rosemary (leaves picked from stem)
- 5 cups Newcastle Brown ale (or other dark ale)
- 2 parsnips (peeled and roughly chopped)
- 2 carrots (peeled and roughly chopped)
- 4 potatoes (peeled and roughly chopped)
- salt to taste
- black pepper to taste
- **For the Dumplings:**
- 1 3/4 cups self-rising flour
- 1/2 cup butter
- 1 pinch salt
- 1 pinch pepper
- 2 sprigs rosemary (chopped)

Directions

1. Season the beef, sprinkle with the flour and toss around until well coated.
2. Heat up a frying pan until it is good and hot, add a little olive oil and fry the beef in 2 batches until nice and brown.
3. Transfer the meat to a big casserole pan -- one that is suitable to go on a stovetop burner -- mixing in the flour that was left on the plate after coating it.
4. Put the casserole on medium heat, add the red onions and pancetta or bacon, and cook until the onions are translucent and the pancetta has a bit of color.
5. Add your celery and rosemary.
6. Now you can pour in your and 1-1/4 cups of water, adding your parsnips, carrots, and potatoes. Feel free to add whatever veg you like at this stage.
7. Bring to the boil, put a lid on, turn down the heat and leave it to simmer while you make the dumplings -- which are a choice.

8. Blitz the dumpling ingredients in a blender or rub between your fingers till you have a breadcrumb consistency, then add just enough water to make a dough that is not sticky.
9. Divide it into ping-pong-ball-sized dumplings and put these into the stew, dunking them under.
10. Put the lid back on and leave it to cook for 2 hours.
11. Taste it, season it as you like, and then serve them with some greens and loads of to mop up the juices.

56.Chicken and Dumplings

Ingredients

- 2 1/2 to 3 pounds chicken (whole or cut up)
- 4 cups water
- 2 cups chicken broth
- 1 carrot (roughly chopped)
- 1 medium onion (cut into quarters)
- 1 stalk celery (roughly chopped)
- 1/2 teaspoon salt
- 1 cup milk
- 1/4 teaspoon pepper
- **For the Dumplings:**
- 2 cups all-purpose flour
- 1/2 teaspoon baking soda
- 1/2 teaspoon salt
- 3 tablespoons shortening
- 3/4 cup buttermilk

Directions

The Chicken

1. Place the chicken in a Dutch oven or stockpot and add the water, broth, carrot, onion, celery, and salt.
2. Bring to a boil, cover and lower heat.
3. Simmer for 60 to 70 minutes, or until the vegetables are tender and chicken is done.
4. Remove chicken to a bowl to cool.
5. With a slotted spoon, remove the carrot, onion and celery pieces from the broth and discard (or add the vegetables back to the broth later with the chicken).
6. Reserve the broth.

7. When the chicken is cool enough to handle, remove the meat from the bones.
8. Discard skin and bones and cut the meat into bite-size pieces. Set aside.

Dumplings

1. In a large bowl, combine the flour, baking soda, and 1/2 teaspoon salt; cut in the shortening with a pastry blender or two knives until mixture is the consistency of coarse meal. Alternatively, mix with a food processor.
2. Add the buttermilk and stir just until dry ingredients are moistened.
3. Turn dough out onto a floured surface and knead 4 or 5 times — no more than that.
4. For drop dumplings, pat the dough down to a 1/4-inch thickness, and pinch off 1-1/2-inch pieces.
5. For rolled dumplings, roll the dough to a 1/4-inch thickness, and cut into 3" x 1" strips.
6. Bring the chicken broth to a boil; stir in the milk and pepper. Correct seasonings, if desired.
7. Drop the dumplings, one or two at a time, into the boiling broth and reduce heat to medium-low.
8. Stir from time to time to make sure dumplings do not stick together.
9. Cook the dumplings for 8 to 10 minutes.

Finishing the Dish

1. Add the reserved cut-up chicken to the mixture and simmer until heated through.
2. Remove from heat.
3. Serve.

57. Italian-Style Goulash Beef Stew

Ingredients

- 1/4 cup lard
- 1 1/3 pounds (500 g) onions, peeled and sliced into rings
- 2 pounds (1 kg) stew beef, cubed
- 1 cup (250 ml) dry red wine (see suggestions, below)
- 1 tablespoon red wine vinegar
- 2 tablespoons paprika
- 2 cups (500 ml) hot water
- 1 bay leaf
- 1 teaspoon ground cumin

- 1/2 teaspoon dried marjoram
- 2 cloves garlic
- Zest of 1 lemon
- The juice of 1/2 lemon
- 1 tablespoon of unsalted butter, at room temperature
- Fine sea salt and freshly ground black pepper, to taste

Directions

1. Gather the ingredients.
2. Heat the lard in a large, heavy-bottomed pot over medium heat and add the onion. Saute, stirring with a wooden spoon, until the onions have softened and browned, about 5-6 minutes. Push the onions to the sides of the pot and brown the cubed beef in the open space in the middle. Mix the meat and the onions together and continue cooking until thoroughly browned.
3. Stir in the red wine and the vinegar, add salt to taste and simmer until some of the liquid has evaporated. Sprinkle in the paprika and add a little of the hot water. Reduce the heat to a slow simmer, cover, and simmer, stirring occasionally, for about 1 1/2 hours. Add more water only as necessary, to keep it from drying out.
4. When the meat is done, remove the onions from the pot and mix them together with the spices, lemon zest, and butter. Return the onion-and-spice mixture to the pot, stir in the lemon juice as well, and cook a few minutes more over low heat. Adjust seasoning to taste with salt and pepper.
5. Serve accompanied with creamy polenta, mashed potatoes, or with wide buttered pasta or egg noodles, and a fairly full-bodied red wine, for example, a Teroldego from Trentino, or a Valpolicella Classico Superiore.

58. Tuscan Wild Boar Stew With Chocolate

Ingredients

- **Marinade** :
- 2 cups red wine
- 1/2 cup red wine vinegar
- 1 medium yellow onion (peeled and halved)
- 1 carrot (coarsely chopped)
- 1 stalk celery (coarsely chopped)
- 1 tablespoon balsamic vinegar
- 1 bay leaf
- 1 sprig fresh thyme (or 1 teaspoon dried)

- 2 teaspoons ground cinnamon
- 2 teaspoons ground nutmeg
- 2 teaspoons ground allspice
- **Stew** :
- 4 tablespoons olive oil
- 1 clove garlic (finely minced)
- 1 medium yellow onion (peeled and finely chopped)
- 1 carrot (finely chopped)
- 1 stalk celery (finely chopped)
- 2 teaspoons dried red chili pepper flakes (or to taste)
- 3 1/2 ounces (100 g) prosciutto (finely chopped)
- 2 1/2 pounds wild boar, stew beef, pork shoulder or other meat (see notes above), cut into 2-inch chunks
- 1 bay leaf
- 1/2 cup dried prunes (plumped in a small amount of warm water, then drained well, coarsely chopped)
- 1 tablespoon brown sugar
- Grated zest of 1 orange
- 1 tablespoon raisins (plumped in a small amount of warm water, then drained well)
- 1 tablespoon pine nuts
- 2 ounces bittersweet chocolate (70% cacao), grated
- Fine sea salt, to taste
- Freshly ground black pepper, to taste
- Garnish: freshly parsley leaves (finely chopped)

Directions

For the Marinade

1. In a large, heavy-bottomed pot, bring all of the marinade ingredients to a boil, then remove from heat and let cool completely. Submerge the chopped raw meat in the marinade and refrigerate, covered, for 48 hours.
2. Strain the meat and vegetables out of the liquid (retaining the marinade liquid). Separate meat from vegetables and discard vegetables and bay leaf.

For the Stew

1. In a large, heavy-bottomed saucepan or Dutch oven, heat the garlic in the olive oil just until it turns lightly golden. Add the onion, carrot, and celery and saute until vegetables are softened and onion is transparent, about 6 to 8 minutes. Add the chili pepper flakes and saute for another 30 seconds. Stir in the prosciutto and saute for about 1 minute.

2. Pat the pieces of meat with a paper towel until dried well, then add to the pot and stir just until browned. Pour in the strained marinade liquid and bring to a simmer, scraping the bottom of the pot with a wooden spoon to loosen any browned bits. Add the bay leaf. prunes and sugar and return to a simmer. Cover and let simmer over low heat until meat is very tender, about 2 hours.
3. When meat is tender, stir in the orange zest, raisins, pine nuts, and grated chocolate. Stir until chocolate is melted and all ingredients are well combined. Taste and adjust seasoning with salt and pepper, as necessary.
4. Serve over creamy bowls of polenta, sprinkled with finely chopped fresh parsley.

59.Manhattan Clam Chowder

Ingredients

- 5 cups water
- 3 dozen clams (quahog or cherrystone clams, scrubbed)
- 5 slices bacon, finely chopped
- 1 large onion (12 ounces) (finely chopped)
- 2 large carrots (peeled and finely chopped)
- 2 stalks celery (finely chopped)
- 1 pound all-purpose potatoes (3 medium) (peeled and finely chopped)
- 1/2 bay leaf
- 1 1/4 teaspoons dried thyme
- 1/4 teaspoon ground black pepper
- 1 (28-ounce) can plum tomatoes
- 2 tablespoons fresh parsley (chopped)
- 3/4 teaspoon salt

Directions

1. In a nonreactive 8-quart saucepot, heat 1 cup water to boiling over high heat. Add the clams and heat to boiling. Reduce heat; cover and simmer until clams open, 5 to 10 minutes, transferring clams to bowl as they open. Discard any clams that have not opened.
2. When cool enough to handle, remove clams from shells and coarsely chop. Discard shells. Strain clam broth through a sieve lined with paper towels into the bowl.
3. In the same clean saucepot, cook bacon over medium heat until browned; add onion and cook until tender, about 5 minutes. Add carrots and celery; cook 5 minutes.

4. Add clam broth to bacon mixture in saucepot. Add potatoes, remaining 4 cups water, bay leaf, thyme, and pepper; heat to boiling. Reduce heat; cover and simmer 10 minutes. Add tomatoes with their liquid, breaking them up with the side of spoon. Simmer 10 minutes longer.
5. Stir in chopped clams and heat through. Discard bay leaf and sprinkle with parsley. Taste for seasoning; add salt as needed.

60. Carbonada Criolla (Argentinian Beef Stew)

Ingredients

- 1/3 cup olive oil
- 1 large onion (chopped)
- 1 green pepper (chopped)
- 2 cloves garlic (minced)
- 1 1/2 pounds stewing beef (cut into 1-inch pieces)
- 1 can stewed tomatoes
- 2 cups beef broth
- 3 sweet potatoes (peeled and cubed)
- 2 white potatoes (peeled and cubed)
- 2 tablespoons sugar
- 1 large winter squash (peeled and cubed)
- 7 ounces dried apricots (roughly chopped (about 1 cup))
- Salt and pepper to taste
- 1 cup frozen corn

Directions

1. Gather the ingredients.
2. In a large pot, heat the oil and sauté the onions, green pepper, and garlic until golden and soft, about 10 minutes.
3. Add the beef and cook on medium-high heat, turning to brown all sides.
4. Add the stewed tomatoes, beef broth, potatoes, sugar, squash and apricots, and lower heat to a simmer.
5. Cover and simmer over low heat for 1 hour. Taste for seasoning, and season with salt and pepper. Add more beef broth if the stew seems too thick.
6. Cook for about 30 minutes longer, until beef is tender. Stir in the frozen corn, and simmer for 5 to 10 minutes more.
7. Serve and enjoy!

61.Curried Beef Stew

Ingredients

- 1 pound lean stewing beef, cut into small cubes
- 1/3 cup all-purpose flour
- 1 scant teaspoon curry powder
- 1/2 teaspoon ground ginger
- 1/2 teaspoon onion powder
- 1/2 teaspoon salt
- dash freshly ground black pepper
- 2 tablespoons vegetable oil
- 2 ribs celery (sliced)
- 1 medium onion (diced)
- 3 cups beef broth
- 1 medium sweet potato (peeled and cut into small cubes)
- 2 medium carrots (chopped)
- 2 small to medium potatoes (peeled cut into small cubes)
- 1/2 cup baby lima beans
- 1 can (14.5 ounces) diced tomatoes with juice

Directions

1. Gather the ingredients.
2. In a plastic food storage bag, combine cubed beef, flour, curry powder, ginger, onion powder, salt, and pepper. Shake to coat the beef and set the bag aside.
3. Heat the vegetable oil in a large saucepan over medium heat. Add the celery and onion; saute until just tender.
4. Add the beef and all excess flour to the celery and onion mixture. Stir well. If necessary, add a little more oil. Continue cooking, stirring, until beef is lightly browned.
5. Add the beef broth; cover and simmer for 30 minutes.
6. Add sweet potato, carrots, potatoes, and lima beans. Cover and simmer for 30 minutes.
7. Add tomatoes. Cover and simmer for 10 minutes longer.
8. Enjoy!

62.Classic Beef Stew

Ingredients

- 3 pounds boneless beef chuck roast (cut into 2-inch pieces)
- 2 tablespoons vegetable oil
- 1 teaspoon salt (plus more as needed)
- Freshly ground black pepper (to taste)
- 2 yellow onions (cut into 1-inch pieces)
- 3 tablespoons flour
- 3 cloves garlic (minced)
- 4 cups cold beef stock or broth
- 3 carrots (peeled and cut into 1-inch pieces)
- 2 stalks celery (cut into 1-inch pieces)
- 1 tablespoon ketchup
- 1 bay leaf
- 1/4 teaspoon dried rosemary
- 1/4 teaspoon dried thyme
- 2 pounds Yukon gold potatoes (peeled and cut into large chunks)
- *Garnish:* fresh parsley (optional)

Directions

1. Gather the ingredients.
2. Season the beef very generously with salt and freshly ground black pepper.
3. Add vegetable oil to a large heavy pot or Dutch oven (one that has a tight-fitting lid), and set over high heat.
4. When the oil it begins to smoke slightly, add the beef and brown very well. Work in batches if necessary.
5. Once well browned, remove the beef to a bowl with a slotted spoon, leaving the oil and beef drippings in the pot.
6. Lower the heat to medium, and add the onions to the pot; sauté about five minutes, or until translucent.
7. Add the flour and cook for two minutes, stirring often.
8. Add the garlic and cook for one minute.
9. Whisk in 1 cup of the beef stock to deglaze the bottom of the pot, scraping up any browned bits caramelized on the bottom.

10. Add the rest of the broth, carrots, celery, ketchup, bay leaf, thyme, rosemary, beef, and 1 teaspoon of salt.
11. Bring back to a gentle simmer, cover, and cook on low for one hour.
12. Add potatoes, and simmer covered for another 30 minutes.
13. Remove the cover, turn up the heat to medium, and cook, stirring occasionally, for another 30 minutes, or until the meat and vegetables are tender.
14. This last 30 minutes uncovered is not only to finish the cooking, but also to reduce and thicken the sauce.
15. If the stew gets too thick, adjust with some more stock or water.
16. Turn off heat, taste and adjust seasoning, and let sit for 15 minutes before serving.
17. Garnish with fresh parsley if desired.
18. Serve and enjoy!

63. Old-Fashioned Beef Stew

Ingredients

- 3 lbs. boneless chuck roast (cut into 2-inch pieces)
- 3 tbsp. vegetable oil
- 2 tsp. salt
- 1 tbsp. freshly ground pepper
- 2 yellow onions (cut into 1-inch chunks)
- 1/4 cup flour
- 3 cloves garlic (minced)
- 1 cup red wine
- 3 cups beef broth
- 1/2 tsp. dried rosemary
- 1 bay leaf
- 1/2 tsp. dried thyme
- 4 carrots (peeled and cut into 1-inch slices)
- 2 stalks celery (cut into 1-inch slices)
- 3 large russet potatoes (peeled and cut in eighths)
- Garnish: fresh parsley

Directions

1. Gather the ingredients.
2. On medium-high heat, add the vegetable oil to a large heavy pot (one that has a tight-fitting lid).

3. When it begins to smoke slightly, add the beef and brown very well. Do so in batches if necessary. Add the salt and pepper as the beef browns.
4. Once browned, remove the beef with a slotted spoon or tongs and set aside.
5. Add the onions and sauté for about 5 minutes, until softened.
6. Reduce heat to medium-low and add the flour. Cook for 2 minutes stirring often.
7. Add the garlic and cook for 1 minute.
8. Add wine and deglaze the pan, scraping any brown bits stuck to the bottom of the pan. The flour will start to thicken the wine as it comes to a simmer.
9. Simmer wine for 5 minutes and then add the broth, bay leaves, thyme, rosemary, and the beef.
10. Bring back to a gentle simmer, cover and cook on very low for about 1 hour.
11. Add potatoes, carrots, and celery and simmer covered for another 30 minutes, or until the meat and vegetables are tender. Taste and adjust seasoning.
12. Turn off heat and let sit for 15 minutes before serving. Garnish with the fresh parsley if desired.

64.Family-Style Crock Pot Beef Stew

Ingredients

- 8 carrots
- 1 1/2 pounds potatoes (about 3 to 4 medium potatoes)
- 2 large onions
- 1 tablespoon vegetable oil
- 2 1/2 lbs. beef chuck
- 2 tablespoons all-purpose flour
- 1/4 teaspoon freshly ground black pepper
- 1/4 teaspoon dried thyme
- 1/4 teaspoon dried basil
- 1/4 teaspoon dried oregano
- 1 (14.5-ounce) can stewed tomatoes (Italian seasoned or regular)
- 2 teaspoons Worcestershire sauce
- Salt (to taste)

Directions

1. Gather the ingredients.
2. Peel the carrots and slice them into 1-inch rounds.
3. Peel the potatoes and cut them into 1-inch chunks.

4. Peel the onions and chop them coarsely.
5. Cut the beef into 1-inch cubes.
6. Heat the vegetable oil in a skillet over medium-high heat. Add the beef and sear until it is well-browned on all sides.
7. Place half of the sliced carrots, potatoes, and chopped onion in the crock pot; top with the beef cubes.
8. In a small bowl, combine the flour, pepper, thyme, basil, and oregano; sprinkle over beef.
9. Add the remaining vegetables then top with the stewed tomatoes and their juices. Sprinkle with Worcestershire sauce.
10. Cover and cook on low for 8 to 10 hours, or until the meat is very tender.
11. Taste and add salt, as needed.
12. Serve the stew with a crusty no-knead bread or buttermilk biscuits.

65.Beverly's Beef Stew With Potatoes

Ingredients

- 2 to 2 1/2 pounds beef chuck
- 2 tablespoons bacon drippings (or oil, or shortening)
- 2 cups onions (chopped)
- 1/2 cup celery (sliced)
- 5 large potatoes (cut into eighths)
- 4 to 5 large carrots (cut into 2-inch slices)
- Optional: kosher salt (to taste)
- Optional: black pepper (to taste)
- Optional: garlic powder (to taste)
- 1 (10.5-ounce) can condensed tomato soup
- 1 1/4 cups water

Directions

Crackpot:

1. Cut the beef into 1-inch pieces.
2. Heat the bacon drippings in a skillet over medium-high heat. Add the beef and cook until browned, stirring frequently. Add chopped onions and sliced celery and cook until tender.

3. Transfer meat and onion mixture, remaining vegetables and seasonings, the soup, and a soup can of water to the crock.
4. Cook on low for 8 to 10 hours or on high for 5 to 6 hours.
5. Check the stew occasionally and add a little water if necessary.

Stove Top

1. Cut the beef into 1-inch pieces.
2. Heat the bacon drippings in a stockpot or Dutch oven over medium-high heat. Add the beef and cook for about 5 minutes, or until well browned, turning frequently.
3. Add chopped onions and sliced celery to the beef and continue to cook until tender.
4. Add the remaining vegetables and seasonings.
5. Add the tomato soup and a soup can of water (or unsalted stock).
6. Simmer over lowest heat for about 2 1/2 to 3 hours, or until meat and vegetables are tender.
7. Add more water or stock as needed.

66.Chili Beef Stew With Beans and Corn

Ingredients

- 2 pounds chuck stew beef
- 2 tablespoons vegetable oil
- 1 cup chopped onion
- 1/2 cup chopped green bell pepper
- 2 cloves garlic, minced
- 2 tablespoons good-quality chili powder
- 1 can/14.5 ounces diced tomatoes, plain, with peppers, or zesty chili-style
- 1 can/4 ounces chopped mild green chile peppers
- 1 cup low sodium or unsalted beef broth
- 1 teaspoon kosher salt, or to taste
- 1/4 teaspoon freshly ground black pepper
- 2 tablespoons all-purpose flour
- 1/4 cup water
- 2 cans kidney beans or small red beans (28 to 32 ounces total)
- 1 can whole kernel corn, drained (approximately 15 ounces)

Directions

1. Cut the beef into 1/2-inch cubes.
2. Heat the vegetable oil a heavy Dutch oven or stockpot over medium-high heat. When the oil is hot, add the beef cubes. Cook, stirring frequently until the beef is browned. Remove the beef with a slotted spoon and drain off all but 2 tablespoons of the drippings.
3. Reduce the heat to medium and add the onion and green bell pepper. Cook, stirring until the onions are translucent.
4. Add the garlic and chili powder to the onion and bell pepper mixture. Continue cooking, stirring constantly, for about 1 minute.
5. Add tomatoes and green chile and then stir in the beef broth, salt, and pepper. Return meat to the pot and bring to a boil. Reduce the heat to low, cover, and simmer for about 1 1/2 to 2 hours, or until meat is tender.
6. Drain the beans — no need to rinse — and corn and add them to the stew mixture. Bring the stew back to a simmer.
7. In a cup, blend the flour with 1/4 cup of cold water; stir into the stew. Cook, stirring constantly until thickened.

67. Crock Pot Beef and Bean Chili

Ingredients

- 1 to 1 1/2 pounds lean ground beef
- 1 cup chopped onion
- 1/2 cup chopped celery
- 1/2 cup chopped green pepper
- 2 (15 1/2-ounce) cans red kidney beans (drained)
- 1 (28-ounce) can tomatoes (diced)
- 1 (6-ounce) can tomato paste
- 1 (4-ounce) can mild green chilies (chopped)
- 2 tablespoons granulated sugar
- 1 large bay leaf
- 1/2 teaspoon garlic powder
- 1 teaspoon kosher salt (or to taste)
- 1 teaspoon dried marjoram (1/2 teaspoon dried oregano)
- 1/8 teaspoon freshly ground black pepper
- Optional Garnish: Shredded cheddar or pepper jack cheese
- Optional Garnish: Cornbread crumble or croutons (see below)

Directions

1. In a skillet over medium heat, cook the ground beef for about 5 minutes. Add the celery, onions, and bell pepper and continue cooking until the beef is no longer pink.
2. With a slotted spoon, transfer the ground beef mixture to the slow cooker crockery insert and add the remaining ingredients.
3. Cover the pot and cook the chili on low for 7 to 9 hours.
4. Remove the bay leaf and stir before serving. Taste and adjust seasonings.
5. Top servings of chili with shredded cheese, cornbread crumble, or croutons, if desired.
6. Serve this chili with cornbread, biscuits, or crackers, as desired.

68. Moshari Kokkinisto or Reddened Beef Stew

Ingredients

- 2 1/4 pounds of lean stewing beef, cut into 5-6 pieces
- 1 1/3 cups of olive oil
- 2 teaspoons of salt
- 1/2 teaspoon of pepper
- 6 cloves of garlic, minced
- 3-4 whole cloves
- 1 pound of onions, diced
- 1 bay leaf
- 1 tablespoon of tomato paste
- 1/2 pound of fresh tomatoes, finely chopped
- 1/2 cup of red wine
- 9 cups of water

Directions

1. Dissolve tomato paste in the red wine.
2. In a large frying pan, brown the meat in hot olive oil. Remove meat from the pan and transfer to a stew pot.
3. Keep the oil hot in the frying pan. Add onions and garlic to the hot oil and sauté until the onions are soft.

4. Add fresh chopped tomato and wine with tomato paste, and cook for a few minutes until it melts, stirring with a wooden spoon.
5. Add the tomato sauce to the meat in the stew pot, and stir in salt, pepper, bay leaf, and cloves.
6. Add a small amount of water and turn heat to high. When it starts to boil, add remaining water slowly, stirring between each addition of water.
7. When it reaches a full boil, cover, reduce heat to medium, and cook for 1 1/2 to 2 hours (test meat for tenderness), stirring occasionally.

69.Stifatho: Beef and Onion Stew

Ingredients

- 3 1/3 pounds/1.5 kilogram of lean beef (cut in egg-sized chunks)
- 3 1/3 pounds/1.5 kilogram of whole boiler onions (peeled)
- 3/4 cups of olive oil
- 3 ounces/6 tablespoons of red wine vinegar
- 10 cloves of garlic (peeled, whole)
- 2 tablespoons of tomato paste
- 2 bay leaves
- 1 stem of fresh rosemary
- 1 tablespoon of salt
- 10 to 12 peppercorns

Directions

1. Gather the ingredients.
2. In a stew pot, lightly brown the meat in olive oil.
3. Add remaining ingredients and enough water to cover, plus 1 inch. Stir to mix with a wooden spoon. Bring to a rolling boil and immediately reduce heat to low. Cover and simmer for 3 to 4 hours without stirring, until only a sauce remains.
4. Serve and enjoy!

70.Crockpot Cider Beef Stew

Ingredients

- 1 1/2 to 2 pounds lean beef stew meat
- 8 carrots (sliced thin)
- 6 medium potatoes (sliced thin)
- 2 apples (chopped)
- 2 teaspoons salt
- 1/2 teaspoon thyme
- 1/2 cup chopped onion
- 2 cups apple cider

Directions

1. Place carrots, potatoes, and apples in the bottom of a slow cooker. Add meat and sprinkle with salt, thyme, and chopped onion. Pour cider over meat.
2. Cover and cook on low heat for 8 to 10 hours.
3. Thicken juices with a flour and cold water mixture (about 1 1/2 to 2 tablespoons flour and 2 tablespoons water), cooking on high in slow cooker until thickened. Alternately, transfer the stew to a large stockpot over medium heat and cook down juices before thickening.

71.Slow Cooker Pork Stew

Ingredients

- 2 pounds pork shoulder (boneless trimmed, cut into 3/4-inch cubes)
- 3 tablespoons flour
- 1 teaspoon salt
- 1/4 teaspoon dried thyme
- 1/4 teaspoon pepper
- 6 carrots (cut into 1/2-inch slices)
- 4 medium potatoes (cut into 3/4-inch cubes)
- 1 cup onion (chopped)
- 1 large apple (peeled, cored, and chopped)
- 2 cups apple cider

- 1 tablespoon vinegar
- 1/2 cup cold water
- 1/4 cup flour

Directions

1. Gather the ingredients.
2. Combine the flour, salt, thyme, and pepper. Toss the spices with the meat.
3. Put the chopped-up vegetables (carrots, potatoes, and onions) and the apple into the slow-cooker.
4. Place the pork cubes on top.
5. Combine apple cider and vinegar, and pour it over the meat.
6. Place the lid on top of the slow cooker and set it on the low setting. Keep it on the low setting for 9 to 11 hours.
7. After that time, turn the slow cooker to high. Blend 1/4 cup flour and 1/2 cup cold water together, stirring them until the mixture is smooth (this will thicken the sauce).
8. Stir the flour and water into the hot liquid. Keep the crock pot on high, and cook it for 15 minutes longer, or until thickened.
9. Taste and adjust seasonings as desired.
10. Serve and enjoy!

72.Crock Pot Spanish-Style Pork Stew

Ingredients

- 1 medium onion
- 1 pound lean pork shoulder (also known as pork butt or Boston butt)
- 4 to 5 medium potatoes
- 1 green bell pepper (or use half green and half red)
- 2 tablespoons vegetable oil
- 1 (14.5 oz) can tomatoes (diced)
- 2 tablespoons vinegar
- 3 garlic cloves (crushed)
- 1 cup chicken stock (preferably low sodium or unsalted)
- 1 bay leaf
- Salt and pepper, to taste

Directions

1. Chop the onion.
2. Cut the pork shoulder into large chunks.
3. Peel the potatoes and cut them into 1-inch pieces.
4. Slice the bell pepper in half lengthwise; remove the stem end along with the seeds and ribs and then slice thinly.
5. Heat the vegetable oil in a skillet over medium-high heat. Add the pork cubes and cook until well browned on all sides, turning frequently.
6. Put the onion in the slow cooker. Top with the browned pork, cubed potatoes, and bell pepper.
7. In a bowl, combine the tomatoes with the vinegar, garlic, chicken broth, and bay leaf. Pour over the pork.
8. Cover the pot and cook the stew on LOW for 7 to 9 hours, or until the pork is tender. Taste and adjust seasonings with salt and pepper, as needed.

73.Pork and Green Chile Stew

Ingredients

- 2 to 2 1/2 pounds pork stew meat, or lean pork, cut in 1" cubes
- 1/4 cup flour
- 1 teaspoon cumin
- 1/4 teaspoon seasoned pepper
- 1 teaspoon salt
- 1 teaspoon ground sage
- 3 tablespoons oil
- 3 tablespoons vinegar
- 2 large onions, coarsely chopped
- 2 cans small whole new potatoes, drained
- 2 or 3 green chiles (such as Anaheim, or what you like), diced, or 1 can (4oz)
- 2 cups tomatillo salsa (salsa verde)
- 1 can (15 oz) chicken broth, reduced sodium
- 1 teaspoon brown sugar

Directions

1. Place flour, cumin, pepper, salt, and sage in a paper bag or food storage bag. Add the pork cubes to the flour mixture and shake to coat thoroughly.

2. Heat the vegetable oil in a large skillet over medium-high heat. Brown the pork in the hot oil in batches; remove when browned and set aside.
3. With the pan still over the heat, add the vinegar to the skillet, scraping up brown bits (vinegar will reduce).
4. Place the onions, chiles, potatoes, salsa, chicken broth, brown sugar, pork, and scraped bits from the skillet in a 5-quart slow cooker. Stir to blend ingredients.
5. Cover and cook on low 8 to 12 hours, or on high 4 to 6 hours.
6. If desired, mash a few of the potatoes to thicken the stew.

74. Slow Cooker Chile Verde- Green Chile and Pork Stew

Ingredients

- 4 pounds of boneless pork, trimmed and cut into bite-sized chunks
- 1 cup chicken broth
- 2 cups green chile sauce*
- 1 cup tomatillos, husks removed and coarsely chopped
- 4 cloves of garlic, peeled and diced
- 1 medium onion, peeled and diced
- 1/4 teaspoon black pepper
- 1/2 teaspoon salt
- 1/2 teaspoon cumin

Directions

1. Place all of the ingredients into the slow cooker.
2. Cook on the medium or high setting for 5-6 hours or on low for 7-8 hours.

*Homemade Chile Sauce Recipe- Roast 2 lbs of fresh green chiles on a grill or under the broiler until the skin is blackened and bubbly. Let them cool, peel the skin off and scrape out the seeds. Cut the stem off and discard the seeds and skin. Puree or blend the chiles with 1/2 cup water, a tablespoon of vinegar and salt to taste (I usually use about a teaspoon) until smooth.

You can also substitute canned green chile sauce if you so desire. You can also add jalapenos for a little added heat. Step-by-Step Instructions to Roast Chiles.

Of course, homemade tortillas are best, but if you need to re-heat some store-bought ones, you can have them steaming hot in just minutes. Place a damp paper or dish towel on a plate, place four tortillas on top, and layer another damp paper towel and more tortillas. Keep layering until you have enough. Microwave the stack for one to two minutes. Remove the tortillas and quickly place in a tortilla warmer to keep them piping hot. They will stay hot for up to thirty minutes. You can also wrap a small stack in a damp towel and place in a 200-degree oven until they are warm which should take 20-30 minutes.

An additional serving option would be to place a warm flour tortilla into a bowl and press it down. Ladle the Chile Verde into the tortilla-lined bowl and serve immediately with toppings and additional tortillas.

75.Carne Adovada: New Mexico Red Chile Pork Stew

Ingredients

- 1 tablespoon vegetable oil
- 3 pounds pork butt (or pork shoulder, well-trimmed of fat and cut into 1-inch pieces)
- 2 onions (chopped)
- 6 cloves garlic (chopped)
- 1 teaspoon fine sea salt
- 1 tablespoon flour (or masa harisa)
- 1/2 teaspoon freshly ground pepper
- 1 cup/8 ounces ground dried New Mexican red chile powder
- 5 to 6 cups water (divided)

Directions

1. Gather the ingredients.
2. Preheat oven to 350 F.
3. Heat a large pot over medium heat. Once the pot is hot, add the oil.
4. When the oil is hot, add the pork pieces to brown them. Add only enough pork so the pieces are in a single layer and don't touch each other; you will likely need to do this in batches. The pork should sizzle the second it touches the pot; if it doesn't, remove it and wait for the pot to heat up.
5. Cook the pork, undisturbed, until each piece is well-browned on one side, about 3 minutes.

6. Turn and brown on all sides.
7. Transfer the pork to a large bowl or plate and repeat with remaining batches as needed.
8. When all the pork is browned and set aside, add the onions, garlic, and salt to the pot. Cook, stirring frequently, until the onions are soft, about 3 minutes.
9. Sprinkle the onions with flour or masa and pepper and cook, stirring, until the raw flavor of the masa or flour cooks off (if you use flour it will smell a bit like pie crust), about 3 minutes.
10. Add the ground chile and stir to combine.
11. Add 4 cups of water and bring to a boil.
12. In a blender, whirl the chile mixture until smooth. You may want to do this in batches, depending on the size of your blender. Only fill the blender about 1/2 to 2/3 full and be sure to hold a kitchen towel over the top to protect yourself (and your walls) from any potential splatters.
13. Return the chile mixture to the pot. If you have a hand-held immersion blender, this is a good time to use it.
14. Once the sauce is blended, add another 1 cup of water and the browned pork and bring everything to a boil.
15. Cover, transfer to the oven, and bake for 1 hour.
16. Take the pot out of the oven and stir the stew after the first hour. Add an additional 1 cup of water to the pot if the stew seems dry.
17. Recover the pot and return it to the oven to bake until the pork falls apart when you try to cut it with a fork and the sauce is thick, about 1 more hour.
18. Serve the carne adovada hot.

90. Perfect Slow Cooker Beef Stew

Ingredients

- 3 slices bacon (chopped)
- 1/4 cup all-purpose flour
- 1 teaspoon salt
- 1/2 teaspoon pepper (freshly ground)
- 2 pounds lean beef stew meat (from round or chuck)
- 8 ounces button mushrooms (cleaned and thickly sliced)
- 1 medium carrot (peeled, thinly sliced)
- 1 1/2 cups frozen pearl onions (thawed)

- 1 teaspoon garlic (minced)
- 1/2 cup dry red wine (such as cabernet sauvignon or pinot noir)
- 1 1/2 cups beef broth
- 2 tablespoons tomato paste
- 1/2 teaspoon dried leaf thyme
- 1/2 teaspoon dried leaf rosemary

Directions

1. In a large skillet or sauté pan over medium heat, cook the diced bacon until almost crisp and fat has been rendered. With a slotted spoon, transfer the bacon to paper towels and leave 1 tablespoon of drippings in the skillet. Refrigerate the bacon; it will be added to the stew near the end of the cooking time.
2. In a food storage bag, combine the flour, salt, and pepper. Add the beef pieces and toss to coat with the flour mixture.
3. Cook the beef in the bacon drippings over medium heat, stirring constantly, until the beef is nicely browned on all sides.
4. Transfer the beef to the crockery insert of a slow cooker. Top with the mushrooms, thinly sliced carrots, and thawed onions.
5. Combine the wine, beef broth, tomato paste, and garlic. Pour over the beef and vegetables. Cover and cook on LOW for 8 to 9 hours or on HIGH for 4 to 5 hours.
6. Stir in the thyme, rosemary, and the reserved bacon. Continue cooking on HIGH, uncovered, for 15 minutes longer.

76.Cuban Beef Stew

Ingredients

- **For the Steak:**
- 2 pounds flank steak (or chuck roast)
- 1 large onion (quartered)
- 2 cloves garlic (smashed)
- 1 large celery rib (chopped)
- 1 tablespoon salt
- **For the Stew:**
- 1/4 cup olive oil
- 2 cloves garlic (minced)
- 1 large onion (sliced into thin strips)
- 1 large green bell pepper (sliced into thin strips)
- 1 1/2 pounds tomatoes (diced)

- 2 tablespoons dry sherry
- 2 bay leaves
- 1 tablespoon ground cumin
- 1/4 cup cooked sweet peas (frozen and thawed are okay)
- Salt and pepper to taste

Directions

Prepare the Steak

1. Place the steak into a large stockpot and add water to cover the steak completely.
2. Add the quartered onion, smashed garlic, chopped celery, and salt.
3. Bring ingredients to a boil, then reduce to moderate heat and cook until steak is tender, about 1 1/2 hours.
4. Transfer the meat only to a platter to cool and discard the cooking liquid, onion, garlic, and celery.
5. Shred it with two forks when the meat is cool enough to handle. At this point, you can refrigerate the meat overnight.

Prepare the Stew

1. In a large skillet or pot, heat the olive oil over medium-high heat. Add the minced garlic and sauté until soft, about 1 minute.
2. Reduce the heat to medium and add the sliced onion and bell pepper. Cook until vegetables are soft, about 10 minutes.
3. Stir in the diced tomatoes, sherry, bay leaves, cumin, and a pinch of salt.
4. Turn the heat to medium-high and cook for 25 minutes, occasionally stirring to prevent sticking.
5. Remove the bay leaves.
6. Stir in the shredded beef and cook for about 10 minutes until the beef is heated through.
7. Stir in the peas. Turn off the heat. Add salt and pepper to taste. Serve immediately with rice if desired.

77.Greek Beef Stew With Orzo Pasta

Ingredients

- 1/2 cup olive oil (divided)
- 3 1/2 pounds beef or lamb (cut into 2-inch chunks)
- Salt and pepper (to taste)
- 1 large onion (diced)
- 4 cloves garlic (finely minced)
- 1 large leek (cleaned, trimmed and cut in half)
- 1 large carrot (peeled and cut into thirds)
- 1/2 cup dry white wine
- 3 to 4 whole allspice berries
- 1 (28-ounce) can crushed tomatoes
- 1 teaspoon sugar
- 1 quart of water
- 1 pound orzo pasta
- Grated kefalotyri cheese or Pecorino Romano

Directions

1. Heat the oven to 350 F.
2. In a heavy, oven-safe Dutch oven or deep pan, heat 1/4 cup olive oil. Season the meat lightly with salt and pepper and cook over medium-high heat until nicely browned about 7 to 10 minutes. Remove the browned meat from the pot and set aside on a platter.
3. Add the remaining 1/4 cup olive oil to the pan and sauté the onions until translucent, about 5 minutes. Add the garlic and cook until fragrant, about 1 minute. Add the leek, carrot, and the wine to the pot and scrape up any bits that may have stuck to the bottom.
4. Add the allspice berries, crushed tomatoes, sugar, and a quart of water to the pan. Let it come to a boil and then lower the heat to medium-low. Simmer uncovered for 5 to 10 minutes.
5. Return the meat (with juices) to the pot. Cover and simmer over medium-low heat for about 1 hour or until the meat is very tender.
6. Remove the leek and carrot from the sauce and transfer the meat and sauce to a covered ceramic baker or continue using the Dutch oven.

7. Stir in the uncooked orzo pasta and add about 1/2 cup more water if needed. Season to taste with salt and pepper.
8. Cover and place in the oven. Cook 45 minutes to 1 hour, stirring the contents occasionally to prevent sticking.
9. Remove from the oven, remove the allspice berries and top with grated cheese. Cover and allow the dish to rest for 15 to 20 minutes before serving.

78.Instant Pot Minestrone Stew

Ingredients

- 1 tablespoon olive oil
- 3 cloves garlic (minced)
- 1/2 onion (diced)
- 4 carrots (peeled and diced)
- 4 celery stalks (diced)
- 1/2 head green cabbage (thinly sliced)
- 1/2 cup prepared pesto
- 1 cup crushed tomatoes
- 3 cups vegetable broth (or chicken)
- 1 cup small shell pasta
- 2 bay leaves
- 1 teaspoon salt
- 1 teaspoon ground black pepper
- 1 (14-ounce) can cannellini beans
- 1 tablespoon parsley (chopped)
- 1/2 cup spinach (chopped)

Directions

1. Gather the olive oil, garlic, onion, and vegetables.
2. Add the olive oil to the Instant Pot insert. Set the pot to sauté and heat the oil. Add the garlic, onion, chopped carrots and celery. Sauté until the vegetables are fragrant and translucent, about 5 minutes.
3. Gather the rest of the ingredients.
4. Add the green cabbage, followed by the pesto, crushed tomatoes, vegetable broth, pasta, bay leaves, and salt and pepper. Set to the soup or broth setting for 3 minutes. Close the lid and make sure to adjust the gauge towards sealing.
5. After the timer goes off, release the steam immediately. Add in the cannellini beans, parsley, and spinach. Set to sauté and heat until the beans and spinach are heated through. Taste and add additional salt and pepper if needed.

6. Remove the bay leaves and serve it immediately with crusty bread and a simple salad.

79.Chinese Daikon, Carrot, and Tomato Beef Stew

Ingredients

- 1 kg. beef flank (or you can use shin and any part of beef that's suitable for a slow cook, cut into big dice)
- 2 tablespoons oil
- 480 g. tomato (vine, chopped roughly)
- 120 g. onion (or 1 medium onion, chopped roughly)
- 10 g. ginger (thin slice)
- 200 g. carrot (peeled it and slice into 2cm thick)
- 600 g. daikon radish (peeled it. Slice into 2cm thick and cut into quarters.)
- 700 ml. water
- **For the Seasonings:**
- 200 ml. light soy sauce
- 1 teaspoon dark soy sauce
- 70 ml. rice wine
- 2 whole star anise
- 1/4 cinnamon stick
- Optional: dried orange peel (for extra flavor)

Directions

1. Boil a big pot of water and add the beef. Boil for 5 minutes to clean any dirt off the beef. After 5 minutes, use cold water to wash away any dirt on the surface of the meat and drain the water. Leave the beef aside for later.
2. Heat up 2 tablespoons of oil and stir-fry the ginger and onion until the fragrance comes out. Add the beef and stir-fry for another 3-5 minutes.
3. Pour the rice wine in and cook for 30 seconds. Add light and dark soy sauce and bring it to boil.
4. After step 3 has boiled, add tomato, water, star anise, cinnamon stick and orange peel (optional).
5. Bring it to boil again and use medium-low heat to simmer for 1.5 hours. Check and stir it often. If you think the water is a bit low in the pot you can add a little bit hot water to adjust it.

6. The beef should be nearly soft after 1.5-hour cooking and then add the carrots and daikon. Cook until the carrots and daikon are soft and this dish is nearly ready. Check the seasonings to suit your taste before serving.

80.Spanish Beef Stew

Ingredients

- 13 ounces/375 g carrots
- 1 yellow onion (medium or large)
- 2 cloves garlic (large)
- 3 tablespoons olive oil
- 1/4 cup flour (all-purpose)
- 1 3/4 pounds/800 g beef (stew meat cut into chunks)
- 8 ounces/250 ml tomatoes (canned, crushed)
- 2 cups/500 ml red wine
- 2 cups/500 ml water
- 1 bay leaf
- 1/2 teaspoon rosemary
- 1/2 teaspoon thyme
- Salt and pepper (to taste)
- 1 to 2 tablespoons flour (all-purpose)

Directions

1. Rinse carrots thoroughly, rubbing off any dirt and debris. Trim off the carrot top. Chop carrots into small pieces (1/4-inch). It is not necessary to peel the carrots.
2. Peel and finely chop the onion and garlic.
3. Pour a few tablespoons olive oil into a large pot or pressure cooker and heat on medium.
4. While oil is heating, spread flour over a large dinner plate. Then, add beef, a few chunks at a time and coat with flour.
5. Add the flour-coated beef to the pot and brown on all sides.
6. Remove beef from pot and set aside.
7. Saute the carrots, onions, and garlic in the same oil (adding a bit more oil if needed so vegetables do not stick).
8. When onions turn transparent, stir in crushed tomatoes.
9. Add browned meat back into the pan.
10. Raise heat to high and add wine, water, and bay leaf.

11. Bring to a boil, then lower heat. Simmer loosely covered for 1 1/2 to 2 hours. Stir occasionally, adding water if needed. Add the rosemary, thyme, salt, and pepper during the last 30 minutes of cooking.
12. Once the meat is cooked, to thicken the broth, remove 1/2 cup of broth from the pot and place into a plastic cup with lid. Stir in 1 to 2 tablespoons of flour. secure the deep brown, and shake until flour is absorbed and there are no lumps. Return mixture to warm stew, stirring until the broth thickens.
13. Serve with boiled or home-fried potatoes.

81.Catalan Beef Stew

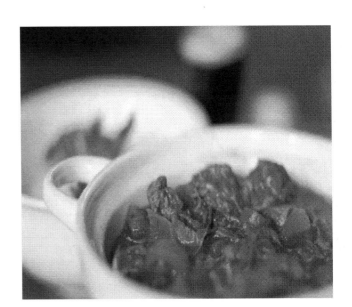

Ingredients

- 1/4 cup Spanish olive oil
- 2 lbs. stew beef, cut into cubes
- 1 tbsp. flour
- 8 oz. glass red wine
- 4 cloves garlic, cut into halves
- 2 onions, chopped
- 2 tomatoes, chopped
- 1 carrot, sliced
- 1 stick celery, chopped
- 1 leek, chopped
- 1 oz. baking chocolate (unsweetened)
- Pinch of cinnamon - about 1/4 tsp.
- Salt and pepper to taste
- 1 1/2 cups beef stock

Directions

This recipe can be made in either a large stock pot or a pressure cooker. If using a pressure cooker, cooking time will be reduced to about 30 minutes.

1. Chop the garlic, onions, tomatoes, carrot, celery, and leak.
2. Pour the olive oil into a large pot with a heavy bottom, or the pressure cooker.
3. Heat the oil and add the cubed stew meat. Brown the meat for 3 to 4 minutes.
4. Add the flour and stir. Add the wine and stir. Cook for 1 minute.
5. Add the garlic, onions, tomatoes, carrot, celery and leak to the pot and stir ingredients.
6. Cut the square of baking chocolate in half and add to the pot.

7. Add beef stock to the pot, stir and bring to a boil.
8. If you are using a standard pot, partially cover and lower to a simmer. Then allow to simmer for an hour to an hour and a half - or until the meat is tender.
9. If you are using a pressure cooker, put on lid and lock. Cook on high pressure for 15 minutes. Remove from heat and allow pressure to drop naturally. This may take 10 minutes. Remove lid and simmer uncovered for another 10 minutes to thicken the stock.

82.Chicken with Rice and Chorizo

Ingredients

- 1 tablespoon olive oil
- 3 pounds chicken thighs (bone-in, skin on; about 6 large thighs)
- salt to taste
- black pepper to taste
- 1/4 pound chorizo (ground uncooked; pork or turkey chorizo)
- 3 leeks (white and light green parts only, sliced)
- 2 teaspoons garlic (minced)
- 1 1/2 cups brown rice (short grain)
- 1 cup white wine
- 2 1/2 cups chicken broth
- 1 cup artichoke hearts (cooked, quartered; canned or defrosted frozen are also fine)
- 1 cup roasted red peppers (diced)
- 1 teaspoon thyme (fresh leaves; see Recipe Tip)
- Garnish: minced fresh parsley

Directions

1. Heat a very large skillet over medium-high heat, and add the oil. Season the chicken with salt and pepper on both sides, then place the chicken skin side down in the pan. Brown the chicken for about 4 minutes, until the skin is golden brown, then turn the chicken and brown the bottoms for another 4 minutes. Remove the chicken to a plate and set aside. Pour off all but 1 tablespoon of the fat left in the pan.
2. Add the chorizo and sauté until the chorizo is cooked through. Transfer that to a small bowl.
3. Add the leeks to the pan and sauté for about 8 minutes, until they are very soft. Add the garlic and sauté for 1 more minute. Add the rice and stir until the rice

is well coated with the leeks and oil. Turn the heat up to high, add the white wine, and cook, stirring occasionally, until the wine is mostly evaporated, about 3 minutes. Add the chicken broth and stir well. Bring the mixture to a simmer and then return the chicken to the pan on top of the rice, skin side up. Cover the pan, reduce the heat so that the liquid stays at a gentle simmer, and cook the rice and chicken for about 40 to 45 minutes until the rice is tender and the chicken is cooked through. The liquid should be almost completely absorbed.

4. About 5 minutes before the rice and chicken are finished cooking, lift the lid, and tuck the artichoke hearts, red peppers and thyme into the rice underneath the chicken. Continue cooking, uncovered, for another 5 minutes.
5. Sprinkle with parsley if desired and serve hot.

83.Rioja-Style Chicken

Ingredients

- 1 chicken (cut into 8 pieces, OR 8 pieces of legs and breasts)
- 1 yellow onion (peeled)
- 2 cloves garlic
- 2 red peppers
- 1 Spanish chorizo sausage
- 3 to 4 tbsp. olive oil
- 2 to 3 sprigs parsley
- 1 cup white wine
- 1 cup chicken broth
- 1 (15 oz.) can peas, drained (or 8 oz. frozen peas)
- Salt (to taste)
- Pepper (to taste)

Directions

1. Gather the ingredients.
2. Peel and chop the onion. Peel the garlic and cut into thin slices. Remove the stems and seeds and cut the red peppers into strips.
3. Slice the chorizo into rounds.
4. Chop the parsley.
5. Heat a large, heavy-bottomed pot with a couple of tablespoons of olive oil. Brown the chicken in the pot on both sides.
6. Remove pot from heat and set aside.

7. While the chicken is browning in the pot, heat 2 tablespoons of olive oil in a large heavy-bottomed frying pan or skillet over medium heat.
8. Add onion and garlic and sauté until onion is translucent.
9. Add parsley, peppers, chorizo. Cook, stirring often for about 10 minutes.
10. Add vegetables to the large pot of chicken and mix.
11. Add white wine and chicken broth. Stir.
12. Cover and simmer for 30 to 40 minutes. About 5 minutes before removing chicken from stove, add peas.
13. Serve and enjoy!

84.Spanish Beef Tomato Stew

Ingredients

- 3 to 4 tbsp. olive oil
- 2 to 2-1/2 lbs. (1 kg.) beef stew meat (in chunks)
- 2 large garlic cloves
- 2 yellow onions (peeled and chopped)
- 1 can (28 oz.) stewed or crushed tomatoes or 5-6 large, fresh, ripe juicy tomatoes
- 1/2 cup white wine or 1/4 cup brandy
- 2 roasted red peppers
- 2 sprigs parsley

Directions

Note: You'll need a wooden or plastic mortar and pestle for this recipe. Why use a mortar and pestle? Using a pestle in a downward circular motion to force ingredients against the surface of the mortar and smashing it will release more flavor than using a food processor. (It doesn't use electricity and it's easier to clean, too!)

1. Gather the ingredients.
2. In a large pot, heat 2 tablespoons of olive oil over medium heat.
3. When hot, add beef and stir to brown on all sides. Make sure that the beef does not stick to the pan. Add olive oil if necessary.
4. Add the chopped onions and sauté on medium to low heat for 5 minutes or so. Add the crushed tomatoes and let cook for 5 minutes.

5. While the beef and tomatoes are cooking, peel the garlic and smash it in the mortar with the parsley. Add a bit of the white wine and swish to clean any garlic and parsley that may be stuck to the inside.
6. Pour contents of mortar and rest of white wine into the pot. Slice the red pepper in half and add to the pot.
7. Stir well. Cover loosely and simmer until the meat is softened. This may take 30-40 minutes. Keep a close eye on the sauce and if it thickens too much, add a small amount of water.
8. Serve with home-fried potatoes or white rice and enjoy!

85.Country Style Beef Stew

Ingredients

- 2 to 3 tablespoons vegetable oil
- 2 pounds lean stewing beef (cut into 1-inch cubes)
- 2 teaspoons salt
- 1 bay leaf
- 1/4 teaspoon dried leaf
- thyme (crushed)
- 1 can (10 1/2 ounces) condensed beef broth (concentrated if using homemade)
- 3 1/4 cups water (divided)
- 4 medium carrots (sliced)
- 2 medium potatoes (cubed)
- 12 small white onions
- 1/4 cup cornstarch

Directions

1. In a large skillet or sauté pan, heat the oil over medium heat. Add beef; brown the meat well on all sides.
2. Add salt, bay leaf, and thyme, along with the condensed beef broth and 3 cups of the water.
3. Cover and bring to a boil.
4. Reduce heat and simmer for 1 1/2 hours. Add carrots, potatoes, and onions; simmer for about 30 minutes longer, or until vegetables are tender.
5. Combine cornstarch and remaining 1/4 cup of water in a small bowl or cup; stir until smooth.

6. Stir the cornstarch mixture into the stew. Bring to a boil, stirring constantly. Boil for 1 minute.

86.Crockpot Beef, Tomatillo, and Green Chile Stew

Ingredients

- 1 1/2 pounds round steak (cut into 1-inch cubes) or lean stew beef
- 1 tablespoon flour
- 1 onion (chopped)
- 2 cloves garlic (minced)
- 2 tablespoons lard or butter
- 4 or more green chile peppers (seeded, chopped), a mixture, mild, hot, your choice
- 1/2 teaspoon dried oregano
- 1/2 teaspoon ground cumin
- 1 cup tomatillo (crushed)
- 1/2 cup beef stock
- Dash of kosher salt and freshly ground black pepper, to taste
- Garnish: fresh cilantro or parsley (chopped)

Directions

1. Dust beef with flour.
2. Brown the beef with onion and garlic in lard or butter.
3. Combine mixture in slow cooker with chili peppers, oregano, cumin, and tomatillos, and 1/2 cup of beef stock (or water).
4. Season with salt and pepper, to taste.
5. Cover and cook on low seven to nine hours.
6. Garnish with cilantro or parsley, if desired, and serve with warm flour tortillas or spoon over rice.

87.All Day Crock Pot Beef and Beer Stew

Ingredients

- 3 pounds stew beef or lean chuck (cut into bite-size pieces)
- 1/2 cup flour
- 1/4 cup butter
- 1 medium onion (sliced)
- 1 teaspoon salt
- 1/8 teaspoon pepper
- 1 clove garlic (minced)
- 12 ounces beer (or use low sodium or unsalted beef stock)
- 1/4 cup flour

Directions

1. Coat the beef cubes with the 1/2 cup flour. Brown in skillet in the butter. Drain off excess fat.
2. In slow cooker, combine browned meat with onion, salt, pepper, garlic, and beer. Cover and cook on low for 6 to 9 hours, or until meat is tender.
3. Turn control to high. Stir the remaining 1/4 cup flour into about 1/4 cup of cold water until smooth.
4. Stir the flour mixture into meat mixture, cook on high for 30 to 40 minutes longer.
5. Serve with rice and salad.

88.Beef and Guinness Stew

Ingredients

- 3 thick slices bacon (diced)
- 1/4 cup all-purpose flour
- 1/2 teaspoon salt
- 1/4 teaspoon ground black pepper
- 2 pounds lean stew beef (or round or lean chuck, cut in 1-inch cubes)
- 2 large onions (chopped, about 2 to 3 cups)

- 1 clove garlic (minced)
- 2 to 3 cups carrots (diced or sliced)
- 1 1/2 cups Guinness stout
- 1 cup beef broth
- 2 tablespoons tomato paste
- 2 teaspoons Worcestershire sauce
- 1 bay leaf
- 1/2 teaspoon dried leaf thyme
- 2 to 3 cups diced potatoes
- 2 tablespoons fresh parsley (chopped)
- Kosher salt (to taste)
- Freshly ground black pepper (to taste)

Directions

1. Gather the ingredients.
2. In a large saucepan or Dutch oven over medium heat, cook the bacon, turning, until lightly browned.
3. In a food storage bag, combine the flour, 1/2 teaspoon of salt, and pepper. Add beef cubes and toss until well coated.
4. Add the beef and onions to the bacon and continue cooking, frequently turning, until beef and onions are browned.
5. Add the garlic and cook, stirring, for 1 minute longer. Then add the carrots, stout, and broth.
6. Stir in the tomato paste and Worcestershire sauce.
7. Add the bay leaf and bring to a boil.
8. Reduce heat to low, cover, and cook at a low simmer for 1 1/2 to 2 hours, or until beef is very tender.
9. Add the thyme and potatoes to the beef mixture and bring to a boil.
10. Cover, reduce heat and simmer for about 30 minutes longer, or until potatoes are tender.
11. Stir in the parsley and add salt and pepper, to taste. Cook for 5 minutes longer.
12. Serve with crusty rolls, biscuits, or slices of freshly baked Irish soda bread.

89.Easy Crock Pot Beef and Mushroom Stew

Ingredients

- 1 1/2 pounds beef chuck (lean, or use round steak)
- 4 (10 3/4-ounce) cans condensed cream of mushroom soup
- 1 (4-ounce) can sliced mushrooms (undrained)
- Optional: dash ground ginger
- 5 cloves garlic (coarsely chopped)
- 1/2 teaspoon dried leaf oregano
- 1/2 teaspoon dried leaf basil
- 1/2 teaspoon onion powder
- 1/4 cup water
- 1/2 teaspoon ground black pepper
- Salt, to taste

Directions

1. Cut the beef into 1/2-inch to 1-inch cubes.
2. Put the beef cubes in the slow cooker along with the condensed soup, mushrooms, ginger, garlic, oregano, basil, onion powder, water, and black pepper.
3. Cover the pot and cook on low for 7 to 9 hours.
4. Serve the beef and sauce with mashed potatoes, rice, or noodles.

91.Anglo-Indian Beef Stew

Ingredients

- 1 kg stew beef, cubed
- 1-liter beef stock
- 3 tbsp vegetable, canola, or sunflower cooking oil
- 2 onions sliced thin
- 2 bay leaves
- 2 star anise
- 6-8 cloves
- 8-10 peppercorns
- 4-5 cardamom pods, split
- 2" cinnamon stick
- 2 tbsp ginger paste
- 3 tbsp garlic paste
- 2 tbsp wheat flour
- 1/2 cup light soy sauce
- 1/2 cup tomato ketchup
- 1 tbsp red chili sauce
- 2 large or 3 medium-sized tomatoes, finely chopped
- 1 cup carrots, cubed
- 1 cup shelled green peas
- 3 large potatoes cut into 4 pieces each
- 1 cup green beans cut into 1" pieces
- 1 cup cauliflower florets
- 1/2 cup radish, cubed
- 1/2 cup pearl onions
- 2 green chilies, slit
- Salt to taste

Directions

1. Set up a deep pot on medium heat. Add the vegetable/ canola/ sunflower cooking oil and heat.
2. Now add all the whole spices and sauté until they are slightly darker and fragrant.
3. Add the onions and fry until golden brown.
4. Add the ginger and garlic pastes and green chilies and fry for a minute.
5. Add the flour and brown, stirring continuously.

6. Add the soy sauce, ketchup, red chili sauce, tomatoes and stir well. Cook till the tomatoes are slightly pulpy.
7. Add the meat and brown.
8. Add the stock, 2 cups of water and the harder vegetables like potato, radish, and carrots and bring the pot to a boil. We do this because the harder vegetables take longer to cook.
9. Cover the pot. Reduce heat to low and cook until the meat is tender. This could take up to an hour. Occasionally check for liquid in the pot and add more if it has reduced too much. Stew must be soupy with plenty of gravy.
10. When the meat is cooked, take the lid off and add the remaining, softer vegetables. Season the Stew with salt and close the pot again.
11. Cook on medium heat till the softer veggies are cooked but not too soft. You will not need to keep checking to ensure you don't overcook them; they must be al dente.
12. While the veggies are cooking, put the cornflour in a cup and add 1/2 a cup of water to it. Stir to mix well and ensure there are no lumps in the mixture. Keep aside to add to the Stew.
13. When the veggies are done, add the cornflour-water mix to the pot and stir. Cook for another minute, allowing the gravy to thicken slightly. Turn off the heat.
14. Serve piping hot with plain boiled rice or crusty bread, if desired.

92.Spanish Beef Stew

Ingredients

- 2 tablespoons extra-virgin olive oil (for sautéing)
- 1 large yellow onion (peel and chopped)
- 3 cloves garlic (peeled and chopped)
- 1/2 green pepper (seeded, membranes removed, and cut into 1-inch pieces)
- 1/2 red bell pepper (or yellow bell pepper, cut into 1-inch pieces)
- Kosher salt (to taste)
- 1 1/2 pounds beef stew meat (cut into cubes)
- 8 ounces crushed tomatoes
- 5 medium carrots (ends trimmed and cut into 1-inch pieces)
- 3 medium potatoes (cut into quarters)
- 1 tablespoon Spanish paprika
- 1 bay leaf
- 1 quart beef broth (or water)
- Freshly ground black pepper (to taste)

Directions

1. Gather the ingredients.
2. Heat a few tablespoons of olive oil in a large pot. Sauté the onion and garlic in the pan.
3. When onion is transparent, add peppers and continue to cook, stirring occasionally.
4. Salt the beef.
5. Add the beef chunks to the onion, garlic, and pepper mixture (also known as a *sofrito*), browning meat on all sides.
6. Add crushed tomatoes, carrots, potatoes, paprika, and bay leaf and stir.
7. Pour in enough water or beef broth to cover ingredients.

Stovetop Method

1. Turn up heat and bring to a boil, then lower heat.

2. Simmer loosely covered for 60 to 90 minutes. Add water as needed, stirring occasionally.

Pressure Cooker Method

1. Lock on top and raise heat to high.
2. When pressure has built up, and it is "hissing," reduce the heat. Cook for 10 to 15 minutes at a steady pressure.
3. Remove from heat and release pressure.
4. Carefully remove the lid and check the meat. Meat should be tender.
5. If further cooking is necessary, add water if needed and secure the lid. After the pressure has built up again, cook another 5 minutes.
6. Serve and enjoy!

93.Slow Cooker Sweet and Sour Beef Stew

Ingredients

- 2 pounds stew beef (cut into 1 1/2-inch cubes)
- 1/4 cup flour
- 1 teaspoon salt
- 1/8 teaspoon pepper
- 2 tablespoons vegetable oil
- 1 cup onion (chopped)
- 6 large carrots (cut into 3/4-inch pieces)
- 1/4 cup brown sugar
- 1/2 cup vinegar
- 1 tablespoon Worcestershire sauce

Directions

1. Mix flour, salt, and pepper; dredge beef in mixture.
2. Heat oil in skillet and brown meat on all sides.
3. Place carrots in bottom of slow cooker; add meat and onions. Combine remaining ingredients and add to slow cooker.
4. Cover and cook on low for 8 to 10 hours. Serve with hot cooked noodles or rice.

94.Beef, Leek and Mushroom Stew

Ingredients

- 2 tablespoon all-purpose flour (on a plate seasoned with salt and pepper)
- 2 tablespoon vegetable oil
- 1 pound rump steak (or braising steak, cut into 1" chunks)
- 3 large shallots (peeled and quartered)
- 3 large garlic cloves (peeled and halved)
- 2 medium leeks (trimmed, cleaned and roughly sliced)
- 1/2 cup red wine
- 1 1/2 pints beef stock
- 6 baby carrots (peeled and cut into large chunks)
- 1 bay leaf
- 5 ounces baby button mushrooms
- salt to taste
- black pepper to taste

Directions

1. Gather the ingredients.
2. Preheat the oven to 300 F
3. Heat the oil in a large frying pan. Pat the beef chunks with a paper towel to make sure they are dry and then add to the frying pan. Stir constantly with a spatula and once browned all over, remove from the pan onto the flour. Stir to lightly coat all the pieces.
4. Place the flour coated beef into an ovenproof casserole dish.
5. Return the frying pan to the heat and add the shallots, garlic, and leeks. Stir and cook for 1 minute.
6. Tip the vegetables from the frying pan into the casserole with the beef.
7. Keeping the pan on the heat add the wine and boil to reduce by two-thirds. While whisking the reduced wine constantly with a hand whisk, slowly add 1 pint of the hot stock. Pour this over the beef and vegetables and stir well.
8. Finally, add the carrot chunks and bay leaf. Stir again.
9. Place the casserole into the preheated oven and cook slowly for at least 2 hours up to 4 hours. Look at the stew from time to time to make sure it hasn't boiled dry, top up with the remaining beef stock as needed.

10. 30 minutes before serving, add the button mushrooms and return the casserole dish to the oven. Cook for a further 30 minutes. Taste and adjust the seasoning with the salt and pepper to taste.
11. Once ready serve with fluffy, buttery mashed potatoes and a green vegetable - cabbage works well, especially the dark green Savoy cabbage.

95.Classic French Flemish Beef Stew

Ingredients

- 2 pounds beef stew meat (cut into 2-inch cubes)
- 2 tablespoons all-purpose flour
- 1/2 teaspoon salt
- 1/4 teaspoon ground black pepper
- 2 tablespoons canola oil
- 2 tablespoons butter
- 4 cups/4 medium yellow onions (sliced)
- 1 clove garlic (crushed and chopped)
- 1 tablespoon brown sugar
- 2 teaspoons dried parsley
- 1 bay leaf
- 1/4 teaspoon dried thyme
- 1 (12-ounce) bottle dark beer
- 1/4 cup to 1 cup beef stock
- 1 tablespoon apple cider vinegar

Directions

1. Gather the ingredients.
2. In a large bowl, toss together the beef, flour, salt, and pepper.
3. Heat the canola oil and butter in a large, roomy pan and brown the beef in it on all sides in batches. If you add all the beef at once it will lower the temperature too much and the meat will boil rather than sear. Carefully watch the beef to make sure it doesn't burn though, but give it enough time to develop a nice, rich brown color–the caramelized sugars will greatly enhance the stew's flavor.
4. Place all the beef back in the pan once browned and add the onions, garlic, brown sugar, parsley, bay leaf, and thyme and stir thoroughly. The onions will pick up a bit of the browned bits in the bottom of the pan.
5. Raise the heat under the pan and stir in the beer and add enough beef stock to cover the beef in the pan. Bring to a boil, then cover the pan, reduce the heat to

low, and simmer for 1 1/2 hours or until the beef is tender. Keep checking to make sure the beef is simmering and not boiling dry. If it seems a little dry, add a touch more stock. The liquid in the pan also should be thickening slightly.

6. Remove the pan from the heat and stir in the apple cider vinegar. Let the stew stand for 10 minutes before serving. Portion into heated bowls with the potatoes and salad on the side.
7. Enjoy!

96.Authentic Mexican Beef Stew

Ingredients

- 6 dried red chiles
- 2 pounds chuck roast
- 1 medium white onion
- 4 cloves garlic
- 1 tablespoon cooking oil
- 2 bay leaves
- 1 teaspoon thyme (dried)
- 1 tablespoon ground cumin
- 1 tablespoon oregano (dried)
- 6 to 8 lime wedges (chopped onion, chopped cilantro and warm tortillas for the side)

Directions

1. Prepare the red chiles by cutting the tops off and removing the stem. We like to use scissors because the dried chiles can be tough. Then, cut a slit down the side of the chile to split it open. The majority of the seeds will shake right out. Use your fingers or a spoon to scrape any additional seeds off and pull off any dried veins.
2. Place the chilies in a bowl and cover it with hot water. They will need to soak 20 to 30 minutes depending on how thick they are. Use a spoon to occasionally push them under the water if they float too much. After you soak the chiles the water will be a brownish color like very diluted coffee. Depending on the chile, it may be bitter or it may have the flavor of the chiles in it, which may be similar in flavor to diluted coffee. If the water is bitter, discard it. If the water has a good flavor to it, you can use it in with the beef broth for extra flavor. Chop the chiles into fine bits. Use a food processor or blender if you want.
3. Cut the beef into 1-inch chunks. We find this easier if the meat is partially frozen or you can have your butcher do it.

4. Peel the onion and discard the papery outer skin. Chop or dice into fine 1/4 inch pieces or smaller.
5. Peel the garlic and crush it or chop it finely.
6. In a large pan, add the oil and begin to saute the onions for about a minute to soften them. Turn the heat to high and add the beef into the pot and turn the pieces often until all of the beef is browned and beginning to get a little crispy on the edges (it doesn't matter if it is cooked all the way through.) Add in the garlic and continue to cook the mixture for another minute. Transfer the cooked beef mixture to your slow cooker and add the beef broth.
7. Add the red chiles, bay leaves, thyme, cumin, and oregano. We start with 1/2 teaspoon of salt and add some later if needed. Turn the slow-cooker to low and let it cook for about 6 hours.
8. Taste the stew and add more salt or seasonings as necessary. Remove the bay leaves and discard them.
9. Serve the stew with fresh chopped onion, chopped fresh cilantro, and a stack of steaming hot tortillas. Serve each bowl with a lime wedge.
10. Enjoy!

97. Crock Pot Beef Stew With Onion Soup Mix

Ingredients

- Optional: 2 tablespoons oil or bacon drippings
- 1 1/2 pounds stew beef (lean, cut into 1-inch cubes)
- 1 packet beefy onion soup mix (like the Lipton brand)
- 1 1/2 teaspoons beef bouillon granules (or base)
- 1 cup water
- 4 medium potatoes (cubed)
- 3 carrots (sliced)
- 1 stalk celery (sliced)
- 1 can whole tomatoes (with juice)
- 1 clove garlic (crushed)
- 2 tablespoons cornstarch
- 1/4 cup water (cold)
- Salt (to taste)
- Freshly ground black pepper (to taste)

Directions

1. Gather the ingredients.
2. If desired, heat the oil or bacon drippings in a large skillet over medium-high heat and then brown the beef cubes.
3. Put the beef (browned or not) in the slow cooker with the onion soup mix, bouillon, water, potatoes, carrots, celery, tomatoes, and garlic.
4. Cover and cook on LOW for 8 to 10 hours, or until the beef and vegetables are tender.
5. Taste and adjust seasonings, adding salt and pepper, as needed.
6. Add 2 tablespoons of cornstarch mixed with the 1/4 cup of cold water.
7. Turn heat to HIGH and stir until thickened.
8. Serve with crusty bread and enjoy!

98. Easy Crock Pot Beef Curry Stew

Ingredients

- 2 tablespoons olive oil or vegetable oil
- 1 1/2 pounds lean stew beef or other lean beef, cut into cubes
- [1/4 cup flour
- 1 teaspoon salt
- 1 teaspoon Creole or Cajun seasoning
- 1/2 teaspoon garlic powder
- 2 medium onions, sliced
- 1 can (14.5 ounces) diced tomatoes, drained
- 3/4 cup beef broth
- 4 teaspoons curry powder, or to taste
- 1 jar (about 12 ounces) small white onions, drained, or frozen pearl onions

Directions

1. Heat the vegetable oil in a large skillet over medium heat.
2. In a food storage bag or shallow bowl, combine the flour, salt, Creole seasoning, and garlic powder; toss beef with the mixture.
3. Add the coated beef to the skillet along with the sliced onions. Cook, stirring, for about 4 to 6 minutes, or until beef is browned and onions are tender.
4. Transfer the beef and onions mixture to a 4- to 6-quart slow cooker. Pour beef broth into the skillet and scrape up any browned bits. Pour over the beef and onions in the slow cooker.
5. Add tomatoes and stir in curry powder and small white onions.

6. Cover and cook on low heat for 8 to 10 hours.

99.Simple Beef Stew

Ingredients

- 2 tablespoons vegetable oil
- 1 pound beef stew meat, cut into bite-size pieces
- 1/4 teaspoon salt
- 4 cups assorted cut-up fresh vegetables (potatoes, carrots, celery, and onions)
- 1 can (14 oz each) lower sodium beef broth
- 1 can (8 oz each) Hunt's® Tomato Sauce with Basil, Garlic and Oregano

Directions

1. Heat 1 tablespoon oil in large skillet or saucepan over medium-high heat. Add meat and salt; cook 5 minutes, stirring until browned on all sides. Remove from skillet; keep warm.
2. Add remaining 1 tablespoon oil and vegetables to skillet. Cook 5 minutes or until crisp-tender, stirring occasionally. Return meat to skillet; stir in broth. Bring to a boil. Reduce heat to medium-low; simmer 15 minutes, stirring occasionally.
3. Stir in tomato sauce; simmer 15 minutes more or until meat and vegetables are tender, stirring occasionally.

100.Classic Homemade Beef Stew

Ingredients

- 1/4 cup all-purpose flour
- 1/4 teaspoon black pepper
- 2 lb. chuck pot roast, trimmed and cut into 3/4" pieces
- 3 tablespoons vegetable oil
- 3 cups vegetable juice
- 3 cups beef broth
- 2 medium onions, cut into thin wedges
- 1 cup thinly sliced celery
- 2 tablespoons Worcestershire sauce
- 1 teaspoon dried thyme
- 1 bay leaf
- 4 red potatoes, cut into 1-inch cubes
- 4 carrots, peeled and cut into 1/4-inch slices on a bias
- 1 1/2 cups frozen peas

Instructions

1. Place the flour and the pepper in a large resealable plastic bag. Add the beef, seal the bag, and shake until all the pieces are coated with the flour mixture.
2. In a 5 to 6 quart Dutch oven or heavy pot, heat half of the vegetable oil over medium-high heat. Add half of the beef and cook until browned on all sides. Remove the beef to a plate, add more oil, and cook the remaining beef.
3. When the beef is browned, return all of the beef to the pot. Stir in the vegetable juice, beef broth, onion, celery, Worcestershire sauce, thyme and bay leaf. Bring to a boil, then reduce the heat and cover and cook for 1 hour.
4. Stir the potatoes and carrots into the stew. Return to a boil, reduce the heat and cover and cook for an additional 30 to 40 minutes, or until the vegetables are tender.
5. Stir in the peas and cook until heated through. Remove the bay leaf and serve.

Conclusion

Stewing is done by cooking together meat, vegetables and other sweet-smelling herbs and flavors in a fluid, generally water or stock, on exceptionally low warmth for quite a while. The nourishment is stewed until it becomes delicate and well-cooked. The fluid (sauce) is served alongside the nourishment that is cooked. Secured pans or cookers ought to be utilized to get ready stewed plans, and the nourishment thing ought to be totally submerged in the delicately stewing fluid. Care ought to be taken not to expand the force of warmth as a lot of warmth may prompt the nourishment getting singed. The mellow warmth and delayed cooking time cause even the hardest slices of meats to get delicate by separating the connective tissue into gelatin. There is no loss of supplements from the nourishment as the solvent supplements are just given from the nourishment to the cooking fluid, which is later served alongside the nourishment. Stewing is a tedious technique for cooking. Stewed plans are commonly a piece of family unit cooking.

Stewing is favorable as in its exceptional upgrades and focuses the regular kind of dishes, and it likewise makes intensely slices of meat simple to process by making them delicate. Hence, by making reasonable and extreme cuts of meat delicate, stewing additionally ends up being a prudent strategy for getting ready nourishment.

Made in United States
Orlando, FL
28 March 2022

16250085R00065